EASY RECIPES FOR WHEN YOU'RE
REALLY F*CKING HUNGRY

TASTY as F*CK

Zoe Gifford

CASTLE POINT BOOKS
NEW YORK

TASTY AS F*CK. Copyright © 2020 by St. Martin's Press. All rights reserved. Printed in the United States of America. For information, address St. Martin's Press, 120 Broadway, New York, NY 10271.

www.castlepointbooks.com

The Castle Point Books trademark is owned by Castle Point Publishing, LLC. Castle Point books are published and distributed by St. Martin's Press.

ISBN 978-1-250-27215-7 (paper over board)
ISBN 978-1-250-27216-4 (ebook)

Cover and interior design by Tara Long
Special thanks to Jennifer Calvert

Our books may be purchased in bulk for promotional, educational, or business use. Please contact your local bookseller or the Macmillan Corporate and Premium Sales Department at 1-800-221-7945, extension 5442, or by email at MacmillanSpecialMarkets@macmillan.com.

First Edition: 2020

10 9 8 7 6 5 4 3 2 1

Contents

— Introduction to —
MAKING SHIT DELICIOUS

EVER LOOK AT A COOKBOOK AND THINK, "Damn, that looks amazing," and then remember that you barely know how to turn on the oven? With *Tasty as F*ck*, your days of missing out on amazing homecooked meals are over! From the Hungover Brunch BLAT to Grown-Ass Mac 'n' Cheese, these recipes are not only tasty as fuck, they're also easy as fuck to whip up. For all you hardcore folks out there who are following specific diets, you'll find plenty in these pages that are gluten free, dairy free, vegetarian, and vegan so you, too, can get in on this fucking great food train. If you read a recipe and think, "oof, that seems like a lot of fucking onions," then go easy on the onions. This book is a judgment-free zone, so you can do you. If you find yourself overthinking things, knock that shit off. (You don't need to know what a dash of salt is. Google knows.) And when all else fails, fucking wing it!

TRUST ME, IT'LL ALL TURN OUT *Tasty as Fuck.*

Chapter One

SHIT
YOU CAN EAT
WITH YOUR
HANDS

Lazy-Ass
LOADED NACHOS

I said this book is a judgment-free zone. That means that if you want to eat a giant fucking mound of delicious, cheese-smothered nachos for dinner, I'm all for it. Hey, the food groups are basically covered—what more do you want? *Technically* this recipe serves two, but let's be real. You're going to house the whole damn plate by yourself, and I don't fucking blame you!

Serves 2

24 or so tortilla chips
(about 2 ounces' worth)

5 ounces pulled rotisserie chicken

1 pinch cumin powder

1 pinch cayenne pepper

1/2 cup canned black beans,
drained and rinsed

1 green bell pepper, stemmed,
seeded, and finely diced

1 jalapeño, stemmed, seeded,
and sliced

3/4 cups shredded
Mexican-blend cheese

Whatever the fuck else you want!

1 Preheat the oven to 375°F and line a baking sheet with nonstick foil (hell yeah, zero cleanup!).

2 Throw the chicken in a zip-top bag with the spices and shake shit up to coat it.

3 Do your best impression of Jackson Pollock and layer the nacho ingredients onto the baking sheet in an eye-catching pattern.

4 Bake it up for 9-11 minutes. That's it! Make your nachos even more fucking amazing by topping them off with some fresh salsa, avocado, and sour cream.

Hungover
BRUNCH BLAT

This sandwich is half egg-and-cheese, half BLT, and completely fucking amazing for soaking up last night's tequila shots. Got leftover French bread from Panera? Use it. Want to sprinkle a little everything bagel seasoning all over it? Abso-fucking-lutely. As long as you follow the basic formula, you can't fuck it up.

Serves 2

8 slices thick, peppered bacon

4 slices Monterey Jack cheese

4 slices thick, rustic white bread

1 medium avocado, smashed

2 slices large heirloom tomato

1 large handful kale

Olive oil spray

2 large eggs

4 tablespoons unsalted butter

1 Line a plate with paper towels. Cook the bacon in a large skillet on medium heat for about 8 minutes, turning it once halfway through, then move it to the paper towel-lined plate to drain off some of the grease.

2 Layer half the avocado, bacon, tomato, and kale onto one slice of bread and add the cheese to the other slice. Repeat with your second sandwich.

3 Fry the eggs: Spray a small, nonstick pan with olive oil and bring it to a medium heat. Crack the eggs into the pan, let them cook until the clear areas turn solid and white, then flip the eggs and let them cook for another 30 seconds or so. The yolks should be runny so that they can soak into the rest of your delicious fucking sandwich, unless runny eggs freak you out.

4 Top your cheese slices with the cooked eggs and close the sandwiches. Add 2 tablespoons of butter to the pan, let them melt, and then move the sandwiches to the pan (carefully, so you don't make a fucking mess). Let the sandwiches toast for 1-2 minutes before adding the rest of the butter to the pan and (again, carefully) flipping the sandwiches over. Your finished sandwiches should be a mouthwatering golden brown with melted cheese and taste like fucking heaven.

Tasty Tip - Here's the trick to great bacon: leave it the fuck alone. You want to let it sit in the skillet untouched for a few minutes like you're searing a good steak, then turn it once. Don't fucking touch it again until done cooking.

If you're a devoted meat eater, don't think of this as vegan food. This is just really great fucking food that happens to be vegan. But I warn you: just one bite could have you swearing off beef altogether. Between the grilled veggies and avocado chimichurri sauce, this "burger" has all the fucking flavor you'll ever need!

1 Prep a grill (or grill pan) with a bit of olive oil and bring it to a medium-high heat.

2 De-stem and clean up the mushrooms, drizzle olive oil over both sides of them, then sprinkle them with the oregano, salt, and pepper.

3 Grill the mushrooms for 10 minutes on each side until they soften and those super fucking satisfying grill marks appear.

4 While the mushrooms cook, prep another large nonstick skillet over medium-high heat. Slice the onion and pepper into 1/4-inch rings, drizzle them with olive oil, sprinkle them with salt and pepper, and then add them to the skillet. Let shit cook, stirring every so often, for 10-15 minutes until the veggies are soft and a little browned.

5 Set the onions and peppers aside, then add the spinach to the skillet. Stir it around for 1-2 minutes until the spinach wilts, then set that aside, too. (And turn off the heat—the cooking part is over.)

6 Add all of the burger sauce ingredients to a food processor and blend them until they're creamy (30 seconds to 1 minute).

7 Spread that delicious sauce onto the buns, build your awesome fucking burger, and enjoy!

✴ Tasty Tip You get burger bonus points if you slather some butter on the inside of the buns and toast them on the grill or in the skillet before assembling all of your ingredients.

Fuck Beef
PORTOBELLO MUSHROOM BURGER

DF | V Serves 2

BEEFLESS BURGER INGREDIENTS

2 large portobello mushrooms

Olive oil

1 teaspoon dried oregano

Salt and pepper

1 medium red bell pepper

1/2 medium red onion, peeled

1 large handful fresh spinach

2 soft burger buns

BEST FUCKING NON-BURGER SAUCE

1 medium avocado

3 medium cloves garlic, peeled

1/4 cup olive oil

1/4 cup fresh flat-leaf parsley leaves

1/4 cup fresh cilantro leaves

Juice of 1 medium lemon

1 teaspoon red wine vinegar

1 pinch red chili flakes

Salt and pepper

Boozy Bitch
BACON CHEESE
FRIES

French fries. Beer-cheese sauce. Bacon. You should probably sit down and take that in for a minute. Maybe have a beer. (Just save a couple tablespoons for your fries.) This recipe is like a night at your favorite pub—except it's better, because you can enjoy it alone, in your house, while wearing onesie pajamas and watching reruns.

Serves 4

2 slices bacon

4–6 cups frozen French fries

Salt and pepper

½ cup low-fat milk

2 tablespoons beer

1 tablespoon cornstarch

1 tablespoon unsalted butter

1 cup grated gouda cheese

⅓ cup shredded cheddar cheese

1 handful jalapeño slices

1 Line a plate with paper towels. Cook the bacon in a large skillet on medium heat for about 8 minutes, turning it once halfway through, then move it to the paper towel-lined plate to drain.

2 Cook the fries according to the directions on the package.

3 Preheat the oven to 375°F. Line a baking pan with some parchment paper for easy cleanup (this shit gets messy), make a layer of fries in the pan, and throw some salt and pepper on them.

4 Make that awesome sauce: In a small bowl, stir together the milk, beer, and cornstarch until the mix is smooth and set it aside. Grab a small saucepan, set the heat to medium, and melt the butter. Then whisk the beer sauce into the butter and let it come to a simmer (little bubbles), stirring now and then. Bring the heat down to medium-low and keep cooking, stirring occasionally, until the sauce thickens up. Once it has, take it off the heat and stir in the gouda. Sauce: done! Pour that delicious shit all over the fries.

5 Crumble the bacon over the fries (using your hands is just easier, and more enjoyable). Next up: all that cheddar and however many jalapeños you can handle.

6 Bake the fries for 5–10 minutes, until the cheese has melted and those fuckers are at peak scrumptiousness. This recipe technically serves 4, but no judgment if you inhale the whole thing by yourself on the couch.

Classy as Hell
BLACKBERRY-PEACH
GRILLED CHEESE

This is not grilled cheese. This is the sweet, mouthwatering heaven of a cheeseboard on buttered toast. This sandwich is so fucking classy, it basically begs to be consumed with a raised pinky and a glass of wine (the good shit—save that screw top for sliders). And the best part is, you can use whatever cheese and fruit you like and it'll still turn out fucking fantastic. Because cheese.

VEG Serves 2

4 tablespoons unsalted butter, at room temperature

4 thick slices sourdough bread

4 tablespoons goat cheese

1 cup blackberries and blueberries

1 peach, thinly sliced

4 ounces fontina cheese, shredded

4 ounces Emmental cheese, shredded

1 drizzle honey (if you want)

1 Heat up a large skillet over medium-low heat. (If you're a fan of toasted sandwiches, a square skillet will make your life infinitely easier!) Slather 1 tablespoon of butter onto one side of each piece of bread, then place the bread butter-side down into the skillet. Reduce the heat to low.

2 Assemble your masterpiece (carefully—burning yourself on a hot skillet sucks): Spread 1 tablespoon of goat cheese onto each slice. In a bowl or on a cutting board, use a fork to lightly mash the berries, then spread them over one of the slices of bread for each sandwich. Top each berry-covered slice with half the peach slices and half of the remaining cheese, then leave it the fuck alone for a minute.

3 When the bottom of the bread is golden brown (use a spatula to peek), close your sandwiches. Then give them a good press with the spatula. Let them cook about 3 minutes on each side until everything is melty, golden deliciousness and you're willing to burn your fucking mouth just to get a piece of it!

Sometimes, you just really want Buffalo wings. OK, all the time. But your arteries will not thank you for eating fried chicken on the regular. Enter: the lettuce wrap. Not only does this shit satisfy that all-consuming Buffalo-sauce craving, it's also gluten free, guilt free, and way fucking easier than making wings. That's probably a bigger win than the score of whatever fucking sporting event you had to pretend to watch to get in on your last batch of tasty wings.

I'm Fucking Craving
BUFFALO CHICKEN
LETTUCE WRAPS

1 In a small bowl, stir up the chicken, cheese, and hot sauce.

2 Fill each romaine leaf with the chicken mix, tomatoes, onion, and a couple of avocado slices.

3 Drizzle some ranch dressing over top of everything and devour all 10 wraps in one sitting (or share with your loved ones, I guess).

GF **Serves 4**

2½ cups shredded rotisserie chicken

¼ cup shredded cheddar cheese

½ cup cayenne pepper sauce

10 leaves romaine lettuce

1 cup halved cherry tomatoes

¼ cup sliced red onion

1 medium avocado, sliced

Ranch, for serving (optional)

Can't Talk, Mouth's Full of PINEAPPLE PULLED-PORK SLIDERS

Put down the damn barbecue sauce. It's time for you to have pulled pork the way it was fucking meant to be—juicy, slow-roasted, pineapple-infused perfection. Throw it on a Hawaiian slider bun, and you're going to have to physically restrain yourself from snarfing whole sammies in a single fucking bite. Trust me, you'll want to savor this shit.

Serves 8

2 1/2 pounds pork shoulder or pork butt

2 medium cloves garlic, minced

1 medium red onion, diced

2 medium red bell peppers, diced

1-2 small jalapeños, diced

1/2 cup soy sauce

1 cup pineapple juice

16 Hawaiian rolls

1 medium pineapple, peeled and cored

1/4 cup fresh cilantro or parsley, for serving

1 Toss everything up to (and including) the pineapple juice into a large slow cooker, then let it do its thing for 4-5 hours on high or 7-8 hours on low. When it's all nice and tender, use a couple of forks to shred it right in the cooker.

2 Preheat the oven to 450°F. Use some tongs to move the pulled pork to a foil-lined baking sheet to create an even layer. Make sure you shake any excess juices into the slow cooker before you do so you don't end up with pork juices all over the damn counter, but don't dump the cooker just yet.

3 Bake the pulled pork for 15 minutes until you start to get that mouthwatering golden-brown coloring. Take the sheet out of the oven, use the tongs to give the pork a good toss, and use a spoon to drizzle some of the juices from the cooker over the pork.

4 Get a nonstick skillet going over medium-high heat while you cut the pineapple into rings, then cut those rings in half. When the skillet's hot, add the pineapple slices and let them cook for a few minutes on each side to caramelize.

5 That's it! Throw some pork and pineapple on some buns with a little bit of tasty greenery on each, maybe drizzle more juices on top if you're feeling it, and enjoy the fruits of your not-so-laborious labor!

 **Tasty Tip** Like your shit spicy? The jalapeño's heat is in its seeds, so make sure you keep them in the mix.

Hotlanta
CHICKEN&WAFFLE
SANDWICHES

Chicken and waffles is a Southern staple for a fucking reason—this shit is good. Like, add it to the roster twice a week good. So, if you don't have a waffle iron, time to suck it up and buy one. You're going to put the damn thing to work!

1 For the waffle batter: Add everything from the flour to the salt to a big bowl and give it a stir. Then add in the rest of the ingredients and mix it all up. Then let the batter sit for 30 minutes while you work on the chicken.

2 Grab three shallow bowls. In one, add the flour. In another, mix together the panko and Cajun seasoning. In the third, stir up the hot sauce, egg, and water.

3 Heat up 3 inches of peanut oil to 375°F in a deep pot or a Dutch oven while you prep your chicken. Remove the tough tendon from each tenderloin (you'll want to watch a YouTube video for this one—it defies explanation), then take the tenders, assembly-line style, through the flour, then the egg mixture, then the Cajun panko. Make sure they're coated at each step.

4 Toss your tenders into the fryer and let them get beautifully fucking golden over 3-5 minutes. Don't crowd them, though—fry in batches if you have to. Transfer finished tenders to a paper towel-lined plate to drain, then sprinkle them with salt and pepper.

5 Preheat your waffle iron and cook your waffles according to its instructions to make 4 large, golden waffles.

6 Once the waffles have cooled, split them up to assemble your sandwiches. (Your chicken-to-waffle ratio is going to depend on the size and shape of your waffle iron.) Top these bad boys with whatever you fucking want while fanning yourself against that heat!

Tasty Tip Whip together the following for a fucking crave-worthy topper: 1 cup mayonnaise, 1/4 cup pure maple syrup, 1/2 teaspoon mustard powder, and 1 teaspoon horseradish.

Serves 4

SCRATCH-MADE WAFFLE BATTER

3/4 cup all-purpose flour

1/4 cup cornstarch

1/2 teaspoon baking powder

1/4 teaspoon baking soda

1/2 teaspoon salt

1 cup buttermilk

1/3 cup peanut oil

1 large egg

1 teaspoon granulated sugar

THAT HOTLANTA CHICKEN

Peanut oil, for frying

1/2 cup all-purpose flour

1 cup panko breadcrumbs

3/4 teaspoon Cajun seasoning

10 dashes hot sauce

1 large egg, beaten

1 tablespoon water

12 chicken tenderloins

Salt and pepper

I'll Make My Own Damn BANH MI

Is it just me, or is banh mi just fucking everywhere? They even have savory-crepe banh mi. And you know what? I'm here for it, because this shit's delish. But if you want to enjoy this Vietnamese delight at home without having to talk to another human, this recipe's for you! (You will need to pick up the ingredients, but that's what headphones and self-checkout are for.)

Serves 1

¼ cup matchstick daikon radish

¼ cup matchstick carrots

1 tablespoon seasoned rice vinegar

¼ cup mayonnaise

1 teaspoon hoisin sauce

1 teaspoon sriracha

1 crusty French sandwich roll

4 ounces cooked pork roast, thinly sliced

2 ounces smooth pâté, thinly sliced

6 thin spears English cucumber, sliced

6 thin slices jalapeño pepper, or more to taste

¼ cup fresh cilantro leaves

1 Preheat the oven to 400°F and line a small baking sheet with some nonstick foil. Throw the radish, carrots, and rice vinegar in a bowl and let that shit marinate for a good 20 minutes.

2 In the meantime, prep your sandwich: Mix up the mayo, hoisin, and sriracha in a small bowl. Open up your roll and spread the mayo mix all over the inside, then move it cut-side up to the baking sheet. Let it crisp up in the oven for about 7 minutes.

3 Use the rest of the ingredients on the list to build your sandwich, then enjoy hearing nothing but the crunch of fresh veggies and crusty bread in the comfort of your own damn house.

The King of All
MOTHERFUCKING
BURGERS

Oh. My. God. This burger. This colossal, mouthwatering, tower of deliciousness. This is everything you never knew you needed in a burger, and you can make it your damn self rather than hitting up that overpriced hipster burger bar down the street. Then all you need is your own microbrew and you can start charging those restaurant prices in your own fucking backyard. (Which is basically the dream, right?)

1 Divide the beef into four equal patties, each about $^3/_4$-inch thick, and sprinkle both sides with salt and pepper. Then stick your thumb into the center of each burger to make a deep depression. (No, seriously. This will puff back up to even out the burger when it cooks.)

2 Set your grill or stove to high heat, brush the burgers with oil, and let them cook undisturbed on the grill or in a pan until they're seared, about 3 minutes. Then flip them and let them sear on the other side for at least 4 more minutes. That will get you medium-rare burgers, but you can keep cooking for medium, etc.

3 If you can multitask, fire up another burner and bring a high-sided frying pan to a high heat. Once it's hot, add your mushrooms, then cook and stir them for 2-3 minutes. Set them aside while you fry the eggs in the same pan with a little spritz of cooking spray.

4 When everything's cooked, slather some butter on the inside of the hamburger buns and toast them on the still-hot grill or pan.

5 Build your badass burgers and enjoy watching everyone make a mess while trying to fit these enormous fuckers into their mouths!

Tasty Tip Add cheese to your burger 1 minute before you finish cooking it so that it's nice and melty.

Serves 4

$1^1/_2$ pounds ground chuck (80 percent lean) or ground turkey (90 percent lean)

Salt and pepper

$1^1/_2$ tablespoons canola oil

$^1/_2$ pound mushrooms (button, shitake, whatever)

4 large eggs

Cooking spray

4 brioche hamburger buns

2 tablespoons unsalted butter

4 slices cheddar cheese (optional)

1 (2-ounce) package microgreens

1 medium red onion, sliced into rings

$^1/_4$ cup chipotle ketchup

Buttery-as-Fuck
LEFTOVER PORK CUBANO

Anyone can throw some fucking lunchmeat and pickles on a sandwich and call it a Cubano. But you are not anyone. You're going to make a melty, golden Cubano that tastes like it came off LA's finest food truck. You can use any cooked pork for this, but if you want the real fucking deal, make the "I Dream of Delicious Fucking Roast Pork" on page 64. Just don't burn the damn bread.

Serves 4

8 ounces thick deli ham

1 pound roast pork, sliced ¼-inch thick

4 (8-10-inch) Cuban sandwich loaves, halved lengthwise

4 tablespoons Dijon mustard

12 Swiss cheese slices

24 bread-and-butter pickles

4 tablespoons unsalted butter, melted

1 Heat up your cast-iron skillet or electric griddle on medium heat. If you're rocking a panini press, you're golden.

2 Throw the ham, pork, and bread (cut-side down) on the grill and get everything a little toasty.

3 Spread some mustard on the inside of each piece of bread, then divide the ham, pork, cheese, and pickles among the four sandwiches and close them up.

4 Use a brush to slather some butter on the outside of each sandwich before it hits the grill. (This shit's crucial. If you don't have a brush, use room-temp butter and spread it on instead.)

5 Working in batches, press the sandwiches onto the hot surface for a few minutes on each side until it's all golden and melty and you can't wait another fucking minute to eat it. (You just have to resist long enough to whip up the others, 'cause eating while other people wait is a dick move.) Slice the sandwiches on the diagonal, and celebrate your restraint by finally giving in.

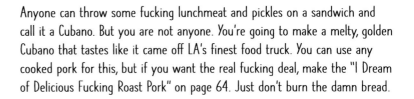

Taco Tuesday will never be the same. Come to think of it, these beautiful veg tacos smothered in cheese and avocado-cilantro-lime crema are just too much for a fucking Tuesday. They've got Self-Care Saturday vibes. You should be journaling your gratitude for tacos while you eat them. Go ahead—feed your stomach and your soul. (But mostly your stomach.)

1 Drain and rinse your black beans, then stir together the black beans, salsa, and spices in a medium saucepan over medium-low heat. Let everything simmer, stirring now and then, for a good 5-10 minutes.

2 In the meantime, dump the crema ingredients into a food processor and pulse (keep hitting the fucking button) until everything's chopped up and creamy.

3 Warm up your tortillas by brushing them with a little olive oil and frying them in a skillet over low heat for a few minutes on both sides until they start to get golden brown in spots.

4 Assemble your tacos with your warm tortillas, black beans, tasty fucking crema, and all that other good shit and get ready to be crowned queen of Taco Sunday.

Extra AF
BLACK BEAN
TACOS
with
AVOCADO-LIME CREMA

VEG Serves 4

WHO NEEDS MEAT?
2 (14.5-ounce) cans black beans

1 cup salsa

1½ teaspoons chili powder

1 teaspoon ground cumin

Salt and pepper

BEST. CREMA. EVER.
½ medium avocado

½ cup plain Greek yogurt

1 cup chopped fresh cilantro

1 tablespoon lime juice

1 large clove garlic, minced

Salt and pepper

OTHER GOOD SHIT
8 (6-inch) corn tortillas

Olive oil

Shredded romaine lettuce

Shredded Mexican blend cheese

Diced tomatoes

Whatever the fuck else you want

Hell Yeah
FALAFEL
WITH TZATZIKI

If your favorite days at the office always seem to coincide with the halal truck showing up outside, this is the recipe for you. Life is too fucking short to wait for that tasty shit to come to you. Now you can brighten up every workday with yummy-as-fuck homemade falafel! Make your own falafel and make those taste buds happy on your off hours.

1 Rinse and drain the chickpeas, then pat them dry before adding them, the garlic, and all the falafel herbs and spices, plus the shallots and seeds, to a food processor. Blend everything together (getting in there with a spatula if you have to) until you have a crumbly dough.

2 Add the flour 1 tablespoon at a time, pulsing the processor as you go, until the dough is way less wet and sticky.

3 Move the dough to a mixing bowl, cover it, and let it sit in the fridge to firm up for 1-2 hours (or the freezer for 45 minutes, for those of us who started prepping dinner too fucking late, again).

4 Scoop the chilled dough by the rounded tablespoon to create about a dozen small discs.

5 Heat the oil in a large skillet over medium heat. Cook the falafels in batches for 4-5 minutes each, flipping them when their bottoms are brown and crispy.

6 Set the finished falafel aside to cool a bit while you whip up the tzatziki by throwing all of its ingredients in a bowl and whisking them together.

7 Assemble your pitas, top them with tzatziki, and savor the flavors of the Middle East.

Tasty Tip Like your falafel extra crispy? Chill the dough in the fridge instead of the freezer, roll the discs in panko, fry them, and then shove them in the oven for 5-10 minutes at 400°F.

VEG Serves 4-6

FALAFEL MAKINGS

1 (15-ounce) can chickpeas

4 medium cloves garlic, minced

1/3 cup chopped fresh parsley or cilantro

1 1/2 teaspoons cumin

1/4 teaspoon each salt and black pepper

1 healthy pinch each cardamom and coriander (optional)

2 medium shallots, minced

2 tablespoons sesame seeds

3-4 tablespoons all-purpose flour

2 tablespoons avocado oil, for cooking

EASY TZATZIKI

1/2 cup Greek yogurt

Juice of 1 large lemon

1 tablespoon extra-virgin olive oil

1 tablespoon freshly chopped dill

Salt and pepper

THE FINAL TOUCHES

Pitas

Chopped lettuce

Sliced red pepper or tomato

Thinly sliced cucumbers

Brag-Worthy
HARISSA-ORANGE
HONEY
HOT WINGS

We all know that it isn't about who wins the game. It's about who brought the best food. And these gorgeous wings will win every fucking time. Bring these bad boys to one party and you're going to be making them for the rest of your life. But you won't mind, because when you *make* the wings, you get to *eat* the wings.

GF | DF Serves 4

SPICE THINGS UP

Cooking spray

1 tablespoon Aleppo pepper

1½ teaspoons salt

1 teaspoon red pepper flakes

1 teaspoon smoked paprika

1 pinch cayenne pepper

Black pepper, to taste

2 pounds prepped chicken wings
(drumettes and flats separated)

THAT GLAZE, THO

¼ cup harissa red pepper spread

¼ cup hot (spicy) honey

Zest of 1 orange

¼ cup freshly squeezed orange juice

2 tablespoons unsalted butter

1 tablespoon fresh lemon juice

Sea salt flakes (optional)

1 Preheat the oven to 425°F, line a rimmed sheet pan with nonstick foil, and place a baking rack on the sheet. Give the rack a good coating of cooking spray.

2 Stir all the wing spices together in a large bowl, add the chicken wings, and toss them around (gently, so you don't get spice mix fucking everywhere).

3 Spread the wings out over the baking rack and bake them for about 40 minutes, using tongs to flip them 20 minutes in, until they're cooked through, crispy, and golden fucking brown.

4 Meanwhile, whip up the glaze: Whisk together the harissa, honey, orange juice, and zest in a small saucepan over medium heat. Let the mixture come to a boil, then reduce the heat to low and let it simmer for five minutes. Take the saucepan off the burner (and turn it off, obviously) and whisk in the butter and lemon juice until everything's nice and smooth and smells fucking delicious.

5 In another large bowl, (gently) toss together the baked wings and the glaze. Serve up these kick-ass wings with a smattering of fancy-ass flaky salt for extra style points.

Tasty Tip Make your life easier and look for chicken wings that are already fucking separated. Trust me.

Here for These
HONEY-BALSAMIC
RIBS

I hear you saying, "but ribs are so much fucking work." Nope. These deliciously sticky ribs will literally take you 10 minutes because your big-ass slow cooker does all the heavy lifting. Meanwhile, you can chill with a glass of wine. (Hey, you have to break out the bottle for the sauce anyway.)

1 Cut up the ribs however you need to fit in your slow cooker (it's OK to layer them).

2 Stir up the lemon juice and all of the rib spices in a small bowl, then use your hands to rub the mixture all over the ribs—like, all over.

3 Add the ribs to the slow cooker, put the lid on, and let that shit marinate for about 30 minutes. Then carefully add the wine, pouring it into the bottom of the cooker so you don't wash away all those tasty fucking spices.

4 Switch the cooker on at low heat and let the ribs cook for 5-6 hours, until the meat's ready to just fucking fall off the bones.

5 Cover a rimmed baking sheet with nonstick foil and use tongs to move the ribs over to it. (Make life easy on yourself and put the baking sheet right up against the slow cooker.)

6 Time to make the glaze: Add 1¹/₄ cups of the cooking juices from the slow cooker to a small saucepan over medium–high heat. Stir in the balsamic vinegar and honey and bring everything to a boil, then lower the heat and let things simmer for 6-8 minutes to thicken up.

7 Move the oven rack to the top position and turn on the broiler. Using a basting brush, brush some of the glaze over the ribs. Pop them under the broiler for 2-3 minutes, then take them out, glaze them again, rotate the pan, and broil them for another 2-3 minutes. This is the only part that requires your fucking attention, so turn off Netflix. Do not burn these damn ribs now.

8 Serve that shit up hot with plenty of extra glaze, and obviously take all the credit for your slow cooker's hard work.

GF | DF Serves 6

FLAWLESS FUCKING RIBS

1 full rack spare or back ribs
Juice of 1 large lemon
1 tablespoon salt
1 tablespoon Dijon mustard
6 large cloves garlic, minced
2 teaspoons onion powder
1 teaspoon dried thyme
¹/₂ teaspoon black pepper
¹/₄ cup red wine or water

TOP 'EM OFF

1¹/₄ cups cooking juices
¹/₃ cup balsamic vinegar
¹/₄ cup honey

Fuck, That's Good,
SPICY FISH TACOS

If fish tacos aren't a sign that heaven is a place on Earth, then I don't know what is. And this slaw-topped take is fucking unforgettable. It also packs some flavorful heat, so for once, leave the sriracha in the damn fridge. If you're feeling especially ambitious, serve these up with some black beans and corn. (Relax, you literally dump them from the cans into a pot.) Make good choices—eat better tacos.

1 Grab a shallow bowl or baking dish for the marinade. In that dish, whisk together the olive oil, lime juice, paprika, chili powder, cumin, and cayenne. (Or just use a fork to stir shit up.)

2 Toss the cod into the mix and let it soak up that marinade for 15 minutes. Meanwhile, whip up the slaw: dump all of the slaw ingredients into a bowl and stir everything up until the cabbage is damn-well covered.

3 Time to cook! Heat the vegetable oil up in a nonstick skillet over medium-high heat. Throw a healthy fucking amount salt and pepper on both sides of each piece of cod before putting it in the pan flesh-side down. Cook the fish for 3-5 minutes on each side until it's totally opaque (i.e., cooked the fuck through). Then move it to a plate or cutting board to chill out for about five minutes.

4 Now, let's make those tortillas nice and fucking toasty: let them cook for 1-2 minutes per side in a clean skillet over medium-high heat. Move the finished tortillas to a plate and keep them covered with a dishrag until you're ready for them.

5 Taco time! If you want to be all fucking civilized, plate some fully assembled tacos (fill the tortillas evenly with the fish, that kick-ass slaw, and avocado and top them with some sour cream and a squeeze of lime). Otherwise, put the toppings on the table and let everyone dig the fuck in!

✱ Tasty Tip Not here for the healthy shit? Skip the marinade and dredge the fish instead for a delicious fucking golden-brown crisp. Just mix the marinade spices with 3/4 cup all-purpose flour in a shallow bowl and toss the fish in it before it goes in the frying pan.

GF **Serves 4**

SOME FUCKING GOOD TACO INGREDIENTS

3 tablespoons extra-virgin olive oil

Juice of 1 medium lime

2 teaspoons chili powder

1 teaspoon paprika

1/2 teaspoon ground cumin

1/2 teaspoon cayenne pepper

1 1/2 pounds cod
(or other flaky white fish)

1/2 tablespoon vegetable oil

Salt and pepper

Olive oil spray

8 corn tortillas

1 medium avocado, diced

Lime wedges, for serving

Sour cream, for serving

KICK-ASS SLAW INGREDIENTS

1/4 cup mayonnaise

Juice of 1 small lime

1 tablespoon freshly chopped cilantro

1/2 tablespoon honey

2 cups shredded purple cabbage

1/2 medium jalapeño, minced

Salt and pepper, to taste

The Perfect Fucking CHICKEN QUESADILLA

Sure, you could throw some chicken and cheese in a tortilla and call it a quesadilla. But that's actually just a "chicken melt" and your boring ass will need some white milk to go with it. This, however, is a fucking quesadilla. This thing packs in the kind of flavor deserving of margaritas and guacamole freshly made with one of those giant volcanic-stone mortar and pestle sets. (That's what that's called, FYI. This book is full service—delicious fucking recipes *and* vocab lessons.)

Serves 4

1 tablespoon extra-virgin olive oil

2 medium bell peppers, diced

1/2 medium white onion, diced

Salt and pepper

1 tablespoon vegetable oil

1 pound boneless, skinless chicken breasts

1/2 teaspoon chili powder

1/2 teaspoon ground cumin

1/2 teaspoon dried oregano

4 medium flour tortillas

2 cups shredded Monterey jack

2 cups shredded cheddar

2 small green onions, thinly sliced

Sour cream, for serving

1 Heat up the olive oil in a large skillet over medium-high heat before adding the peppers and onions. Sprinkle them with salt and pepper, cook them until they soften up (about 5 minutes), and then set them aside.

2 Add the vegetable oil to the same skillet and let it heat up while you season the chicken breasts with salt, pepper, chili powder, cumin, and oregano. Then slice them into strips, add them to the hot pan, and let them cook (stirring now and then) for about 8 minutes, until they're cooked through and golden. Set the chicken aside with the onions and peppers.

3 Place a flour tortilla in that same hardworking skillet and top half of it with a quarter each of the cheeses, chicken, onion-pepper mixture, and green onions. Fold the empty half over the loaded half and let your delicious creation cook for about 3 minutes per side until everything's all toasty and melted. Then do the same thing three more times.

4 Slice your quesadillas into wedges, serve them up with some salsa, sour cream, and guac, and bask in the glory of everyone asking you for your perfect fucking quesadilla recipe.

Crushing My Meal Prep
GREEK CHICKEN KEBABS

If you think these kebabs are lemony perfection hot off the grill, just wait until you throw this shit in with your Sunday meal prep. It's a fucking game changer. Feeling extra lazy? Skip the side-dish prep and thread your veggies straight onto the skewers. Lemon-spritzed zucchini, peppers, red potatoes—all options that no one at work can bitch about having to smell. Honestly, you might make some new friends.

GF | DF **Serves 4**

1/4 cup olive oil

1/4 cup freshly squeezed lemon juice

1 1/2 teaspoons sea salt

1 1/2 teaspoons dried oregano

1/2 teaspoon dried rosemary

1/2 teaspoons black pepper

1 pinch cayenne pepper

3 large garlic cloves, minced

1 pound boneless, skinless chicken breasts

Olive oil, for cooking

Lemon chunks, for presentation

10-inch skewers

1 Throw everything from the olive oil to the garlic into a small bowl and whisk it all together.

2 Chop the chicken up into bite-size chunks, then add them to a large zip-top bag. Then pour the marinade into the bag, seal it, and squish things around until the chicken is good and coated. Let that shit marinate for no less than 1 hour. (Overnight is better.)

3 When you're all set, grab a 12-inch skillet (or larger) with a fitted lid. Add a little olive oil to the skillet and let it get hot over medium-high heat.

4 Thread your chicken pieces and lemon chunks onto the skewers however you fucking want. When the oil is hot, add the skewers to the skillet, cover them with the lid, and let them cook for 5-7 minutes before you fucking touch them to get a good sear. Then continue turning and cooking them on all sides, which should take another 15 minutes altogether.

5 Let the chicken rest for a few minutes before serving it up to super-impressed guests (or putting three servings in the fridge for later so that you don't have to eat another depressing desk lunch).

Tasty Tip This one's not so much a tip as a fucking requirement. If you're using wooden skewers, you either soak them in water for at least an hour before grilling or you *will* set shit on fire.

Chapter Two

SUNDAY FUCKING DINNERS

Sriracha-Makes-Everything-Better MEATLOAF

Raise your hand if you can't get enough fucking sriracha! (Are you actually raising your hand? You realize I can't see you, right?) This ain't your mama's meatloaf. This is the meatloaf they'd serve at Sriracha Fan Club membership meetings, if that were a thing. Which it should be. Because this shit's delicious.

1 Preheat the oven to 375°F while you whip up the sriracha glaze: stir all three ingredients together in a small bowl. (You'll use some of this in the meatloaf and some on top.)

2 Cut the bread into ¼-inch cubes, spread them out over a baking sheet, and let them toast in the oven for a few minutes. Keep an eye on them, though. You want them toasted, not fucking burned.

3 Break out a large bowl and a whisk to combine everything from the Worcestershire to the sriracha glaze—i.e., not the meat or bread.

4 Now it's time to get your hands dirty! (It's just fucking easier this way.) Crumble the meat and bread into the bowl a bit at a time. So, half of the beef, some bread, half of the turkey, some bread, the rest of the beef, some bread, the rest of the turkey, the last of the bread. This might seem fucking insane, but it really does result in a mouthwatering meatloaf. Get in there with your hands and gently smoosh everything together until you have a good-looking meatloaf mix. (I promise you'll find this oddly satisfying. Just wash your fucking hands before and after.)

5 Now move your meatloaf mixture into its 9 x 5 loaf pan, flatten the top, and poor the rest of the sriracha glaze over it nice and even.

6 Bake your meatloaf for 1 hour, then take it out and allow it to rest on the counter for 10 minutes. I know it smells good, but restrain yourself.

7 Using potholders, carefully tilt the pan over a bowl or the sink to drain any excess fat or juice. Then slice, serve, and just try not to eat the whole thing in one go—this makes bomb AF leftovers.

DF **Serves 6–8**

SRIRACHA GLAZE
1½ cups ketchup

1½ teaspoons apple cider vinegar

2 tablespoons sriracha

AMPED UP MEATLOAF
2 slices potato bread

2 tablespoons Worcestershire sauce

1 large egg

2 teaspoons salt

½ teaspoon black pepper

1 teaspoon sweet paprika

4 medium cloves garlic, minced

8 sprigs fresh thyme, leaves stripped and chopped

½ cup chopped Vidalia onion

1 large green onion, minced

½ cup sriracha glaze

1 pound ground chuck, divided

1 pound ground dark meat turkey, divided

Butter Me Up
BUTTER CHICKEN

Butter chicken is the perfect dish—fight me. It's so innocuously tasty, and it's the fastest way to fall in love with Indian food if you aren't already. But it has all of those crave-worthy Indian flavors, so before you know it, you're hooked and going broke working your way through every Indian restaurant in town. Time for a tasty intervention! This recipe is easy as fuck and will scratch the itch without breaking the bank.

Serves 4

1 tablespoon olive oil

1 tablespoon unsalted butter

1 medium onion, diced

1 teaspoon minced ginger
(or ginger paste)

2-3 medium cloves garlic, minced

$1\frac{1}{2}$ pounds boneless, skinless chicken breasts

1 (6-ounce) can tomato paste

1 tablespoon garam masala

1 teaspoon chili powder or paprika

1 teaspoon fenugreek

1 teaspoon cumin

1 teaspoon salt

$\frac{1}{4}$ teaspoon black pepper

1 cup heavy cream

1 Grab a big skillet or a medium saucepan (anything with enough room that shit doesn't spill out) and set it on medium–high heat. Throw in the oil, butter, and onions, and let them cook for 3-4 minutes, until they get a little golden.

2 Stir in the ginger and garlic and keep stirring for 30 seconds, unless you like burned garlic.

3 Slice the chicken into $\frac{3}{4}$-inch chunks before adding it, the tomato paste, and all the spices to the pan. Cook everything for 5-6 minutes so that the chicken is cooked through.

4 Slowly stir in the cream, then let everything simmer and marinate for 8-10 minutes, stirring now and then, until you can't stand it anymore.

5 Serve that delicious shit with basmati rice or naan (or both—I'm all for double carbs).

Tasty Tip OK, yeah, this dish is a little indulgent. If you're feeling guilty, you can sub half and half or yogurt for the heavy cream. But I highly recommend just leaving your fucks out of the kitchen instead.

Screw the Colonel, MY CHICKEN IS BETTER

Once you taste this freshly homemade southern-fried chicken, you'll never want that heat-lamp-warmed fast-food crap again. This shit tastes like sunshine and self-respect. (The instructions look intense, but here's the gist: marinate, dredge, fry. Super fucking easy.)

1 Season your chicken all over with 1 teaspoon of the seasoned salt and $1/2$ teaspoon of the black pepper before moving it to a baking dish for marinating. Pour $2^1/2$ cups of the buttermilk over the chicken, then flip the chicken to make sure the buttermilk touches everything. Let the chicken marinate in the fridge overnight, flipping it once if you think of it.

2 Half an hour before you're ready to get cooking, take the chicken out of the buttermilk and toss the milk. Grab two shallow bowls, a rimmed baking sheet with a baking rack, and a large cast-iron skillet or Dutch oven.

3 In one of the bowls, stir together the flour, cornstarch, 2 teaspoons of seasoned salt, 1 teaspoon of black pepper, garlic powder, onion powder, and paprika. In the other bowl, whisk together the eggs, $1/2$ teaspoon salt, the last $1/2$ teaspoon of black pepper, $1/2$ cup of buttermilk, and hot sauce.

4 Preheat the oven to 200°F, then add the oil to the skillet until it's $1/3$ of the way full and turn the heat up to medium-high. While that heats up, dredge the chicken in the flour, then the egg mixture, then the flour again.

5 When the heat reaches 350°F, fry the chicken in batches of white meat and dark meat by carefully lowering the chicken into the oil. (Break out the tongs and long sleeves for this. That oil's fucking hot.) Cook each piece for 10-15 minutes per side; the juices should run clear and the internal temp should be 165°F. Keep finished pieces warming on the baking rack in the oven while you finish up.

6 Let the chicken rest for 10 minutes before tearing into it like a damn honey badger.

Tasty Tip "Divided" just means the same shit's used more than once in a recipe.

Serves 8

1 whole fryer chicken, cut into 8 pieces (or just buy 8 individual pieces of whatever the fuck you like)

$3^1/2$ teaspoons seasoned salt, divided

2 teaspoons black pepper, divided

3 cups buttermilk, divided

3 cups all-purpose flour

$1/2$ cup cornstarch

1 teaspoon garlic powder

1 teaspoon onion powder

1 teaspoon paprika

3 large eggs

$1/2$ teaspoon salt

1 teaspoon cayenne pepper sauce

Peanut oil, for frying

A Whole Fucking
ROAST CHICKEN
with
GARLIC-HERB BUTTER

You are a grown-ass adult. Now put on your big-kid pants and roast this fucking chicken. You may want to take some selfies while you do, though. This recipe uses all the best shit—butter, lemon, wine, and garlic—so your guests will think you conned them and bought a rotisserie bird.

1 Preheat the oven to 430°F and spritz a roasting pan with cooking spray.

2 Get rid of the giblets and give the chicken a quick rinse inside and out. Use paper towels to pat the chicken dry, then smother it with the olive oil, melted butter, wine, and lemon juice. Use a heavy hand to sprinkle salt and pepper inside and out, then top things off with a dusting of parsley.

3 Get in there with your bare hands and rub the garlic all over the chicken, including under the skin, which will also help all that other good shit to sink in.

4 Peel the papery stuff off the head of garlic, cut off the top third of it, and stuff it into the chicken with the rosemary and lemon half. (If the garlic won't fit, cut it in half.) Then tie the legs of the chicken together using kitchen twine. (No twine? Better to skip it altogether than to try any lifehacks.)

5 Move the chicken breast-side-up into your roasting pan, pop it in the oven, and let it cook for about an hour and 15 minutes, basting (spooning the juices over top) halfway through.

6 Your chicken is done when you poke the thigh with a knife or a skewer and the juices run clear. Baste it one more time, then broil it for 2–3 minutes to get that gorgeous golden-brown color.

7 Take your beautifully fucking roasted chicken out of the oven, cover it with foil, and let it rest for 10 minutes before carving it up and melting into a puddle of buttery, garlicky happiness.

GF **Serves 4**

Cooking spray

1 (4-5 pound) chicken, room temperature

3 tablespoons olive oil

$1/4$ cup unsalted butter, melted

$1/4$ cup dry white wine

1 large lemon, halved

Salt and pepper

2 tablespoons chopped fresh parsley

4 medium garlic cloves, minced

1 head garlic

3 fresh rosemary sprigs

Tasty Tip Google "rinsing chicken" and you're going to find some serious fucking opinions. Do it anyway, then sanitize your sink.

Sit-on-Your-Ass
SPAGHETTI
& MEATBALLS

Listen, no one's going to judge your lazy ass if you make spaghetti using a jar of sauce and some meatballs from the freezer section. (Especially if you chuck the packaging into the neighbor's recycling bin and tell your dinner guests you slaved over a hot fucking stove all day.) But here's a secret someone's sweet little Italian grandmother won't tell you: scratch-made sauce is actually super fucking easy to make. Just throw some shit in a slow cooker and enjoy the smell of roasting garlic and tomatoes while you sit your ass on the couch and binge-watch shows for four hours.

1 Add all of the meatball ingredients except the olive oil to a large bowl. Using clean hands, get in there and mix shit up until everything is well combined. Then roll the mixture into 2-inch meatballs (you should end up with 15 to 18 meatballs). Embrace the mess, but then wash your damn hands and clean under your fingernails.

2 Line a plate with paper towels and heat the olive oil in a large skillet over medium-high heat. Add the meatballs to the skillet in batches and get that nice brown color on all sides (about 2-3 minutes per batch). Transfer your browned meatballs to the paper towel-lined plate to drain.

3 Next up: the sauce. Dump all of the sauce ingredients into a large slow cooker and stir to combine, then add those delicious fucking meatballs. Cover the pot and let that garlicky goodness cook on low for 7-8 hours or high for 3-4 hours.

4 All that's left to do is cook that spaghetti. Stir it into the sauce about half an hour before you're ready to eat, then cover the pot and let it cook on low for 30-40 minutes, stirring it once somewhere in the middle of that time, until the spaghetti is al dente (a.k.a. edible). Stir in the basil for some fancy flavor and bask in the glory of having made another great fucking meal!

Tasty Tip Grab a jar of minced garlic from the store and you'll be set for all sorts of recipes. (The foodies might skewer me for this one, but mincing garlic is a real pain in the ass. Why complicate shit?)

Serves 6

DELICIOUS FUCKING MEATBALL INGREDIENTS

1 pound lean ground beef

$1/2$ pound Italian sausage, casing removed

$1/2$ cup panko breadcrumbs

$1/4$ cup whole milk

1 large egg, lightly beaten

3 tablespoons freshly grated Parmesan

3 tablespoons chopped fresh parsley

2 medium cloves garlic, minced

Salt and pepper

$1^1/2$ tablespoons olive oil

SCRATCH-MADE SAUCE INGREDIENTS

1 (28-ounce) can crushed tomatoes

1 (15-ounce) can diced tomatoes

1 (15-ounce) can tomato sauce

1 cup beef stock

$1/2$ medium sweet onion, diced

3 medium cloves garlic, minced

2 teaspoons granulated sugar

Salt and pepper

THE FINISHING TOUCHES

8 ounces spaghetti, broken in half

$1/3$ cup chopped fresh basil leaves

Fuck Pot Roast, I'm Making
TUNA POKE BOWLS

Looking for something a little different for Sunday dinner? This spicy tuna poke bowl is fire. Literally. There's a lot of fucking sriracha in here. But if you're not here for the heat, you can skip the sriracha mayo and just enjoy some straight-up delicious Hawaiian culinary culture.

GF Serves 2

SRIRACHA MAYO— NEED I SAY MORE?

2 tablespoons light mayonnaise

2 teaspoons sriracha sauce

YAAAS, SUSHI-STYLE TUNA

1/2 pound sushi-grade tuna, cut into 1/2-inch cubes

2 tablespoons tamari (Not GF? Soy sauce works.)

1 teaspoon sesame oil

1/2 teaspoon sriracha

ALL THAT OTHER GOOD SHIT

1 cup cooked white sushi rice

1 cup sliced Persian cucumbers

1/2 medium avocado, sliced

1/4 cup red cabbage

1 teaspoon black sesame seeds

Tamari, for serving (if you want)

Sriracha, for serving (if you're a sriracha-loving beast)

1 Make that mayo: Literally just mix the mayo and sriracha together. Maybe add a little water if you want to be fancy and drizzle it.

2 In a pretty big bowl, toss the tuna with the soy sauce, sesame oil, and sriracha.

3 Grab your serving bowls (the ones you're going to eat out of) and divide your tuna and all that other good shit between them. Top things off with some of that sriracha mayo, and revel in your crazy fucking culinary skills. (Who the hell makes poke bowls? You do, badass!)

Tasty Tip Raw fish not your thing? Try using imitation crab meat instead. Then it's like everyone's favorite California Roll in a bowl. (And it's a lot fucking cheaper.)

I'm Only Cleaning One Fucking Pot
CREAMY TUSCAN
SHRIMP

One-pot meals are the fucking best. You might have lots of ingredients, and you might work in stages, but at the end of the meal, your over indulged ass only has to wash one thing. Or throw that thing in the dishwasher. And I swear that makes the food taste better. (Also, probably, having all those awesome fucking flavors cooking in the same place.) This dish is no exception, and it makes some super fucking tasty shrimp!

1 Prep the shrimp by peeling them, deveining them, and removing the tails (or better yet, buy it this way), then sprinkle salt and pepper all over them. Add the oil to a large skillet over medium-high heat. Once the oil is shimmering (yes, that's a thing oil does, and you'll know it when you see it), add the shrimp and let them sear for 2 minutes before flipping them and cooking them until they're opaque/done.

2 Set the shrimp aside, reduce the heat to medium, and add the butter. When it's melted, stir in the garlic (and keep stirring) for about 1 minute. Now add the cherry tomatoes and throw a little more salt and pepper into the skillet. Continue cooking and stirring until the tomatoes look ready to burst, then stir in the spinach until it wilts.

3 Slowly stir in the heavy cream, then the Parm and basil, before bringing the mixture to a simmer. Reduce the heat to low and continue to let everything simmer and the sauce reduce for about 3 minutes.

4 Pour the shrimp back into the skillet, give everything a stir, and let it simmer until the shrimp is nice and hot again. Sprinkle some basil and lemon juice over your shrimp before serving it and brace yourself for the fucking barrage of compliments.

GF Serves 4

1 pound shrimp

Salt and pepper

2 tablespoons extra-virgin olive oil

3 tablespoons unsalted butter

3 medium cloves garlic, minced

1$\frac{1}{2}$ cups halved cherry tomatoes

3 cups baby spinach

$\frac{1}{2}$ cup heavy cream

$\frac{1}{4}$ cup freshly grated Parmesan

$\frac{1}{4}$ cup thinly sliced basil

1 lemon wedge

Better-Than-Botox
VEGAN CURRY
IN A HURRY

You don't need complicated recipes adding to your worry lines (those fuckers multiply like gremlins in a shower as it is). So unfurrow that brow and enjoy a dish that not only tastes fucking amazing but also basically cooks itself. You can't do anything about your boss being a dick, but you can let the simmering of spices and the mouthwatering Indian-Thai fusion of flavors melt away your worries for the next few minutes.

GF | DF | V | VEG
Serves 4

1 tablespoon olive oil

1 cup chopped cauliflower

1 medium green onion

1 medium sweet potato

2 medium carrots

1/2 medium zucchini

2 sticks lemongrass

2 teaspoons curry powder

1 tablespoon yellow curry paste

1 can full-fat coconut milk

1 (15-ounce) can chickpeas, drained and rinsed

Juice of 1 lime

1 tablespoon maple syrup

1/2 teaspoon salt

1 Add the olive oil to a large pan over medium heat. While that's warming up, chop up the sweet potato, carrots, spring onion, cauliflower, and zucchini. Add the veggies to the pan and fry them for 5-7 minutes.

2 Ready to have some fun? Beat the lemongrass with a wooden spoon. (No, I'm not fucking with you. It loosens up the juices.) Stir that, along with the curry powder and paste, into the veggies and let everything cook for 2 more minutes. Next, add the coconut milk, chickpeas, lime juice, maple syrup, and salt. Let the curry simmer for another 5 minutes, stirring now and then.

3 Take out the lemongrass, squeeze some extra lime over everything if you want, and serve up your fancy vegan fare over some basmati rice. (Or the leftover rice from last night's Chinese takeout. Whatever.)

Tasty Tip OK, I'm going to give you one tiny thing to worry about—double-check your curry labels for fish derivatives. They sneak in sometimes.

Fancy AF
BROILED COD
IN ONE PAN

Sure, this dish is impressive. Blood orange, almond-crusted fish, swanky vegetables—this shit is high-class all the way. But the best thing about it is how little fucking effort it takes. Throw everything on a foil-lined baking pan, let it bake, then toss the foil. In the end, you've got zero cleanup and a meal so fancy that your guests will feel underdressed.

GF Serves 4

1/4 cup mayonnaise

1/4 teaspoon red pepper flakes

2 medium garlic cloves, minced, divided

2 teaspoons finely grated orange zest, divided

1 teaspoon salt, divided

4 (6-ounce) skinless cod fillets

1 medium fennel bulb, thinly sliced

1 bunch broccolini, trimmed and halved

1 small orange, preferably blood, thinly sliced

1 (15.5-ounce) can white beans, drained and rinsed

2 tablespoons olive oil

1 tablespoon fresh rosemary leaves

1/4 cup sliced almonds, chopped

1 Preheat your oven to 350°F. In a small bowl, stir up the mayo, red pepper flakes, 1 teaspoon of the garlic, 1 teaspoon of the orange zest, and 1/2 teaspoon of the salt.

2 Line a rimmed baking sheet with nonstick foil (scrubbing pans is for suckers) and place the cod fillets on the foil. Spread the mayo mixture evenly over each piece of fish.

3 In a large bowl, toss together the fennel, broccolini, orange slices, beans, oil, rosemary, and the last of the garlic, orange zest, and salt. Pour this mixture onto the baking sheet around the fish and cover the whole thing with foil.

4 Pop the baking sheet into the oven and let things cook for 15-20 minutes. Then remove the foil, turn the heat up to broil, and let everything cook for up to 5 minutes more, until the fish is golden-brown on top.

5 Remove the baking sheet from the oven, top the fish with almonds, and put it back under the broiler for another minute or so until they crisp up. Then plate up your gorgeous fucking meal and break out the wine to wash away the Sunday scaries.

Tasty Tip Cook time can depend on how thick your fish and veggies are. Trust your gut and add/reduce time accordingly.

I've got nothing against gnocchi that's smothered in marinara and cheese. And when I say, "nothing against," I mean I will eat that shit all day every day. But at least once in your life, you have to enjoy your gnocchi the way nature intended-fried in oil and garlic until it's golden and toasty. And by "once in your life," I mean all the fucking time, because you will never get enough of this pasta.

GNOCCHI
the Way They're Fucking Meant to Taste

1 Heat the oil in a medium skillet over medium heat, stir in the garlic for about a minute, then toss in the gnocchi and make sure to give it some fucking breathing room.

2 Sprinkle some salt and pepper over the pasta with the red pepper flakes (go easy if you're heat sensitive-those little bastards pack a punch), and let it cook for 8-10 minutes, stirring now and then, until they're beautifully golden and crisp.

3 Throw the gnocchi in a bowl for now and add the mushrooms to the pan. Cook them for about 3 minutes until they're soft, then return the gnocchi to the pan along with the tomatoes, spinach, and beans. Stir everything until the spinach wilts and everything's nicely warmed through.

4 Throw some mozz on top if you want, then take a moment to contemplate how much fucking faster that was than going all the way to a restaurant and waiting for someone else to make it.

VEG Serves 4

2 tablespoons olive oil

1 teaspoon minced garlic

1 (18-ounce) package gnocchi

Salt and pepper

$1/4$-$1/2$ teaspoon red pepper flakes

2 cups mushrooms, sliced

$1/3$ cup diced sundried tomatoes

4 cups loosely packed spinach

1 (19-ounce) can white beans, drained and rinsed

Shredded mozzarella (optional)

Farmhouse-Fucking-Chic
SKILLET CHICKEN POT PIE

Chicken pot pie is just the ultimate fucking comfort food. It's one of those dishes that warms you up from the inside out. But you know what isn't heartwarming? Fucking with piecrust and making a mess of it. That's why you're just going to drop some biscuits on the damn thing and call it a day. And screw roasting a chicken—that's what rotisserie is for. Same hearty, homemade taste, and way less fucking effort!

1 Preheat the oven to 375°F and make sure the rack's in the middle.

2 Grab a large cast-iron skillet and melt some butter over medium heat. When it gets foamy, stir in the veggies and spices, then partially cover the pan with a lid. Let things cook for 5-6 minutes to soften up, then stir in the flour.

3 Whisk in the chicken stock and let things thicken up for a minute, then reduce the heat to low and stir in the milk, mustard, and nutmeg.

4 Next up: prep the chicken. Remove the skin (no judgment if you need to eat a couple of bites of chicken with the skin while you prep) and pull/cut off enough chicken to fill 5-6 cups. Then remove the bay leaf from the skillet and stir in chicken, lemon juice, lemon zest, and peas.

5 While that simmers for a minute, quarter 8 biscuits (that means four pieces per biscuit, if you're too dazed by the smell to read the damn directions at this point). Drop the biscuit chunks evenly over the skillet, then pop the whole skillet into the oven and let it bake for 20-25 minutes.

6 Drizzle some hot honey over your fancified chicken pot pie with the flourish it fucking deserves!

Serves 4

4 tablespoons unsalted butter

1 large sweet onion, chopped

2 medium carrots, chopped

2 large ribs celery with tops, chopped

4 medium cloves garlic, minced

1 medium leek, chopped

Salt and pepper

1 large dried bay leaf

2 tablespoons fresh thyme

1 rounded tablespoon all-purpose flour

2 cups chicken stock

1 cup whole milk

2 tablespoons Dijon mustard

1/8 teaspoon nutmeg

1 rotisserie chicken

1/2 large lemon, juiced and zested

3/4 cup frozen peas

1 tube large buttermilk biscuits

Hot honey, for topping

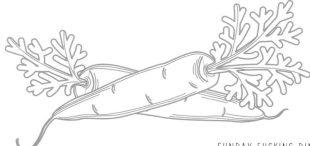

Bomb-Ass
DRY-RUBBED
BRISKET

Are you always asked to bring the salad to the Sunday barbecue? Yeah, that's not because you're known for your excellent salad-making skills. It's because no one trusts you with the fucking meat. Bring this bad boy to the next get-together and your friends and family will be singing a different tune—through brisket-glazed lips.

DF **Serves 8**

2 tablespoons chili powder

2 tablespoons salt

1 tablespoon garlic powder

1 tablespoon onion powder

1 tablespoon ground black pepper

2 teaspoons dry mustard

1 dried bay leaf, crushed

1 tablespoon granulated sugar

4 pounds beef brisket, trimmed

1½ cups beef stock

1 Preheat your oven to 350°F while you prep your dry rub. In a small bowl, stir together all of the spices and sugar. (A little sweetness with the heat makes all the fucking difference!)

2 Use those hands to rub the spice mixture all over the brisket, then move it to a roasting pan.

3 Cook the brisket, uncovered, for 1 hour before adding the beef stock to the pan. Then lower the temp to 300°F, cover the pan tightly with foil, and let it cook for another 3 hours until it's ready to melt in your fucking mouth.

4 Trim away any fat, slice the meat across the grain, top it off with some of the juices from the pan, and then get your damn hands out of the way before your frenzied guests stick you with a fork.

Tasty Tip Make sure the seal on that foil is tight as fuck if you want the most melt-in-your-mouth tender brisket.

Mellow as Hell
MUSHROOM RISOTTO

Risotto is basically just a fancy name for "cheesy, wine-infused rice," and who the hell can't get behind that? It goes with everything! Veggies, chicken, shellfish, bacon—risotto can do no fucking wrong. This one uses a simple combo of mushrooms and herbs for a warm, hearty, rainy-Sunday vibe. You may have heard that making risotto is a pain in the ass, but I don't think stirring qualifies as hard labor. Just put on a fucking podcast and relax.

GF Serves 4

8 cups low-sodium chicken or vegetable broth

1 tablespoon extra-virgin olive oil

1 medium onion, finely chopped

2 tablespoons unsalted butter, divided

2 medium cloves garlic, minced

1 pound mushrooms, sliced

1 dried bay leaf

Leaves of 4 sprigs thyme

Salt and pepper

2 cups Arborio rice

1/2 cup white wine

1 cup freshly grated Parmesan

2 tablespoons chopped fresh parsley

1 Add the broth to a medium saucepan over medium heat, bring it to a simmer, then reduce the heat to low.

2 Grab a big pot or Dutch oven to cook the risotto in, add the oil to it, and warm it up over medium heat. Add the onion and stir until it's translucent, about 5 minutes.

3 Stir in 1 tablespoon of the butter, plus the garlic, mushrooms, bay leaf, and thyme, and cook everything for another 4 minutes or so, until the mushrooms are soft and golden. Throw some salt and pepper in there, then pour the mixture into a bowl, cover it, and let it hang out while you cook the rice.

4 In the same pot, melt the second tablespoon of butter and stir in the rice. Keep cooking and stirring until the rice is all buttery and smells kind of toasty, about 2 minutes. Then stir in the wine and let it cook until the rice has absorbed most of it.

5 Ladle in about a cup of the broth and keep stirring intermittently until most of it's been absorbed. Then do it again (and again), until the risotto is cooked and creamy but not a mushy mess. You can just ditch any unused broth.

6 Stir the mushroom mixture back into the risotto and let it warm up again while you stir in the Parm. Top it off with more Parm and some parsley before serving it up to your guests, who will immediately start doing the "we're not worthy" bow. Probably.

Faster-than-Fucking-Takeout CHICKPEA TIKKA MASALA

One pot. Half an hour. All the fucking flavor of your favorite Indian chicken dish with none of the meat. That sounds (and tastes) like a fucking win to me. You'll need to stock up on some Indian spices if you don't have them, but don't let that scare you off. Once you taste this shit, you'll be reaching for those spices on the regular.

GF | DF | V | VEG
Serves 4

2 tablespoons extra-virgin olive oil

1 medium onion, diced (approx. 1½ cups)

1 teaspoon fine sea salt

2 jalapeños, cored and finely chopped

2 tablespoons minced ginger

4 medium cloves garlic, minced

1 teaspoon garam masala

1 teaspoon ground cumin

1 teaspoon curry powder

½ teaspoon smoked paprika

1 pinch cayenne pepper

3 tablespoons tomato paste

2 (15-ounce) cans diced fire-roasted tomatoes

1 cup vegetable broth

1 (15-ounce) can chickpeas, drained and rinsed

1 cup unsweetened coconut milk

Cilantro, for serving (optional)

1 Add the oil to a large pot over medium heat. Toss in the onion and salt and let it cook for about 3 minutes while you stir. (Don't go crazy—a lazy stir will do.)

2 Stir in the jalapeño, ginger, and garlic and let everything cook for another 2 minutes before adding the spices and the tomato paste to the mix. Let shit cook for another 2 minutes, then pour in the tomatoes (juice and all) and vegetable broth. Bring your base up to a boil and let it cook for 10 minutes, giving it a quick stir now and then.

3 Turn the heat down to low to let things simmer, then stir in the coconut milk and chickpeas. Once those warm up, you're good to go! Serve this vegan wonder with basmati rice and sprinkling of cilantro. (And have some naan ready to cut the heat for the bitch babies.)

Tasty Tip Want to know how to make anything more impressive? Garnish it. Doesn't matter what the fuck you use. Parsley, basil, lemon, kale—just throw some extra shit on the plate, call it a garnish, and your meal has instant charisma.

Can you even imagine lasagna without noodles? Of course not. The name literally refers to the type of noodle used in the fucking dish. But you're a rebel in the kitchen, and you do what you want. And what you want is to make some fucking lasagna that even your vegetarian and gluten-sensitive friends can enjoy. If you're serving some notoriously pain-in-the-ass guests, just call it lasagna and leave it at that. Between all the layers of veggies, sauce, and cheese, they won't even know the fucking difference.

We-Don't-Need-No-Fucking-Noodles
VEGGIE LASAGNA

GF | VEG Serves 6

4 medium zucchinis

3 medium Japanese eggplants

2 tablespoon olive oil

$1/2$ teaspoon salt

$2^{1}/_{4}$ cups marinara sauce

$1/2$ cup ricotta cheese

$1/2$ cup grated mozzarella cheese (or as much as you fucking want)

1 tablespoon thinly sliced fresh basil, for serving

1 Preheat your oven to 425°F while you cut the zucchini and eggplant lengthwise into 1/4-inch-thick slices.

2 Toss the zucchini and eggplant in the olive oil and salt in a large bowl. Spread the veggies out on two baking sheets and pop them in the oven for 10 minutes.

3 Grab an 8 x 8 baking dish and spread 1/4 cup of the marinara over the bottom of it. Veggie lasagna isn't worth burning off your fingerprints, so let shit cool before you start layering on the veggies. Start with 4 slices of eggplant, then 1/4 cup marinara, then dot everything with ricotta. Next, lay 4 zucchini slices in the opposite direction (so they cross the eggplant), then the marinara and ricotta again. Keep going until you're out of veggies and top everything off with a last layer of marinara and the mozzarella.

4 Bake the lasagna in the oven for 20 minutes, and make sure that cheese is nice and bubbly.

5 Let your lasagna rest for 10 minutes before tossing some fresh basil on top and serving that shit up to grateful vegetarians who are just so fucking sick of perfectly good pasta being covered in meat.

Tasty Tip Can't fit two baking sheets side by side in your oven? You could get a new oven. Or you could just place the racks on the top rung and the bottom rung, then swap your baking sheets halfway through the cook time to even shit out.

Wholesome-as-Betty-White
CHICKEN LASAGNA

If you thought that lasagna made with beef and marinara was the only way to go, you're in for a fucking treat. Much like Ms. Betty White, this creamy, cheesy, chicken-and-spinach lasagna will delight your senses and warm your soul. It's the perfect dish to share with friends while you catch up and commiserate at the kitchen table—or to serve as an apology for fucking with them a little too hard. (Those *Golden Girls* were mischievous as fuck.)

Serves 6

IRRESISTIBLE LASAGNA SAUCE

3 tablespoons unsalted butter

2 teaspoons minced garlic

3 tablespoons all-purpose flour

$2^{1}/_{2}$ cups whole milk

Salt, to taste

$^{1}/_{4}$ cup grated Parmesan

4 ounces cream cheese, softened

4 cups baby spinach

LASAGNA BUILDING BLOCKS

$^{3}/_{4}$ cup ricotta cheese

1 large egg

8 dried lasagna noodles, cooked or no-cook

2 cups cooked and shredded chicken

2 cups shredded mozzarella

$^{1}/_{4}$ cup grated Parmesan

1 Preheat the oven to 400°F and grease an 8 x 8 baking dish (i.e., butter it, oil it, or spray it).

2 Whip up that delectable sauce: Add the butter to a medium saucepan over medium heat. Once it's thoroughly melted, stir in the garlic and flour for about 30 seconds. Now, slowly whisk the milk into the pan (meaning, a little at a time). Let the mixture come to a simmer and cook until it's thickened up. Take the pan off the heat and throw in the Parm, cream cheese, and spinach. Stir shit up until the spinach wilts, then put the sauce aside for a minute.

3 Lasagna time! In a small bowl, whisk together the egg and ricotta and get ready to layer shit up. The pattern goes: $^{1}/_{4}$ cup of the sauce, 2 lasagna noodles (taking up the width of the dish), $^{1}/_{4}$ cup of the ricotta mixture, $^{2}/_{3}$ cup of the chicken, $^{2}/_{3}$ cup of the mozz, and 1 tablespoon Parm. Start the next round with $^{1}/_{2}$ cup of the sauce and repeat the pattern twice, ending with sauce and Parm. (Notice those last two switched positions. That's so you get a nice crust on top.)

4 Bake the lasagna for 20-25 minutes, making sure the sauce is bubbling before it comes out of the oven. Then let it rest for another 15-20 minutes before serving it up with charming stories of St. Olaf.

I Dream of Delicious Fucking
ROAST PORK

This isn't your ordinary roast pork. This shit is like a vacation for your mouth, complete with tropical drink. You will dream about this pork (probably while you let it marinate overnight). And then you'll book a trip to Cuba for the food because you can't get enough of this flavor. Although it's probably cheaper just to double the recipe. And then use the leftovers for the Cubanos on page 20. Hint, hint.

GF | DF Serves 6

3/4 cup fresh orange juice

1 cup cilantro, finely chopped

1/4 cup finely chopped mint leaves, lightly packed

8 medium cloves garlic, smashed

3/4 cup extra-virgin olive oil

1 tablespoon orange zest

1/2 cup fresh lime juice

2 teaspoons dried oregano

2 teaspoons ground cumin

3 1/2 pounds boneless pork shoulder

Salt and pepper

1 Toss the orange juice, cilantro, mint, and garlic into a food processor, and pulse until everything's well chopped. Pour this mixture into an extra-large zip-top bag along with the oil, orange zest, lime juice, oregano, and cumin. Add the pork to the bag, zip it up, and stick it in the fridge overnight, and let it infuse your fucking dreams with flavor.

2 Preheat your oven to 425°F and grab a rimmed baking sheet with a baking rack. Move the pork to the rack and ditch the marinade. Shake salt and pepper all over the pork (more than you think you need), then shove it in the oven to bake for 30 minutes.

3 Turn the oven down to 375°F and let the pork roast for another hour and a half until it's cooked through (it should reach an internal temp of 160°F).

4 When it's done cooking, move the pork to a cutting board and cover it with foil. Let it rest for a good 20 minutes before carving it against the grain and resisting the urge to put every fucking piece in your mouth before it can make it to the table.

Tasty Tip This recipe calls for crushed garlic, not minced. Use the edge of your knife to press the garlic and release its juices—don't fuck around and really throw your shoulder into it.

PASTA PRIMAVERA

Worth Braving the Farmers' Market

Farmers' markets are great in theory: sunshine, fresh produce, free samples. But then you remember how fucking crowded those things get and that everything you cook comes from a box anyway. Well, it's time to break out a couple of the 95 reusable totes you own and steel yourself for some social interaction. This dish takes fresh veggies to the next level. Just make sure you prep properly (have your ingredients ready to go), and the actual cooking part will be as easy as it is with that boxed shit.

1 Bring a large pot of water to a boil, throw a little salt in it, and then pour in the penne. Let the pasta cook, stirring now and then, for about 11 minutes.

2 While that's cooking, grab an extra-large skillet and warm up the olive oil over medium-high heat. Add the onion and cook it for 2-3 minutes, until it softens up.

3 Throw in the asparagus, mushrooms, and squash, and cook (and stir) everything until it's just tender, about 5 minutes more.

4 Stir in the tomatoes, carrot, garlic, oregano, black pepper, salt, and red pepper flakes, and let everything cook for another minute or so, until the tomatoes start to soften.

5 Your penne should be about done now. Drain it and toss everything together in a big-ass serving bowl with 1/4 cup of the Parmesan cheese. Top each dish with a little more Parm (if you take one thing from this book, it's basically "always add more cheese") and a spritz of lemon juice before devouring it.

Tasty Tip Little-known fact: Parmesan cheese is not vegetarian. (If you must know why, Google it. But you can live a full life without knowing this bit of trivia.) If you want to make a dish like this full-veg, just skip the Parm. You can always throw in a few crumbles of feta or something instead.

Serves 4

Salt, for pasta water

2 cups whole-grain penne pasta

1 tablespoon olive oil

1/2 cup chopped onion

1 pound fresh asparagus, trimmed and cut into 2-inch pieces

2 cups sliced fresh mushrooms

1 small yellow summer squash, halved lengthwise and sliced

2 cups halved cherry tomatoes

1/2 cup shredded carrots

2 medium cloves garlic, minced

1 tablespoon chopped fresh oregano

1/2 teaspoon black pepper

1/4 teaspoon salt

1/8 teaspoon red pepper flakes

1/2 cup freshly grated Parmesan

Lemon wedges

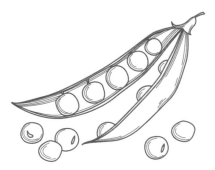

ONE-POT PASTA
with Fucking Superpowers

You know that feeling you get after you eat a big bowl of pasta? That kind of sedentary, foggy-brained food coma that settles in? Imagine eating pasta with ingredients so fucking powerful that they not only counteract the coma but actually give your brain and body a boost. Oh, and the whole thing tastes fucking amazing. I'm not screwing with you—this skillet-cooked chickpea-and-kale pasta checks all those boxes. (You can use any sort of pasta you want, but orecchiette is pretty fucking cool looking.)

VEG **Serves 4**

2 tablespoons olive oil

$1/4$ tablespoon chopped shallot

3 medium cloves garlic, finely chopped

8 ounces orecchiette pasta

$2^{1}/_{2}$ cups vegetable broth

$1/4$ cup low-fat milk

1 teaspoon dried oregano

1 teaspoon basil

$1/4$–$1/2$ teaspoon red pepper flakes

1 cup chopped broccoli florets

$1/2$ cup halved cherry tomatoes

1 (15-ounce) can chickpeas, drained and rinsed

3 cups chopped kale

Salt and pepper

Fresh parsley, for serving

1 Add the oil to a large skillet (with a lid, for later) and warm it up over medium-high heat. Then add the shallot and garlic and cook (and stir) them for a minute or two, until fragrant (i.e., they smell really great).

2 Pour in the pasta, broth, and milk, plus the oregano, basil, red pepper flakes, and broccoli. Let the pasta come to a boil, then cover the skillet, reduce the heat to low, and let shit simmer for 9 minutes.

3 Uncover the skillet, stir in the tomatoes and chickpeas, and let the pasta cook for another 6 minutes. Finally, stir in the kale, and continue stirring here and there while it wilts, the liquid gets (mostly) absorbed, and the pasta finishes cooking, which should all take 4-5 more minutes.

4 Top things off with a sprinkle of salt, pepper, parsley, and more red pepper flakes (if you dare), then serve this up with some salad and crusty bread. (Technically there's already kale in the pasta, so do you need a salad? Maybe just more bread.)

Dad-Joke-level- CHEESY STUFFED SHELLS

The only thing better than pasta topped with cheese is pasta stuffed with cheese. It's just math. Shells give you way more surface area for cheese, and more cheese is always better. Unless you're lactose intolerant. Then you'll probably want to skip this recipe. Buy hey, your call.

1 Preheat your oven to 350°F and grease a 9 x 13 baking dish with some cooking spray. Spread half the marinara over the bottom of the dish and set it aside.

2 Fill a large pot with water, throw some salt in it, and bring it to a boil. Toss in the pasta shells and let them cook for about 3 fewer minutes than the box says to (it'll finish cooking in the oven and you don't want mushy pasta). Drain the shells, rinse 'em off, and set them aside for now, too.

3 In a large bowl, stir up the cottage cheese, Parm, egg, garlic, parsley, basil, salt, and pepper. Use a spoon to fill the shells up with the cheesy mixture before putting them in the baking dish stuffing–side up.

4 Smother the shells with the rest of the sauce and all of the mozzarella before shoving them into the oven to bake for 25 minutes. When they come out, the cheese should be all hot and bubbly (much like yourself, I'm sure).

Serves 6-8

Cooking spray

12 ounces jumbo pasta shells

Salt, for pasta water

30 ounces whipped cottage cheese

6 ounces grated Parmesan

1 large egg

1-2 medium gloves garlic, minced

1 tablespoon freshly minced parsley

3/4 cup freshly chopped basil leaves

1/2 teaspoon salt

1/2 teaspoon black pepper

28 ounces marinara sauce

8 ounces grated mozzarella

Chapter Three

EASY, IMPRESSIVE SHIT

Buh-Bye Postmates Guy
SHRIMP STIR-FRY

If the Postmates guy looks like he's getting a little sick of seeing your front door and footy pajamas, it might be time to try making some takeout favorites at home. This shrimp stir-fry could not be fucking easier. In fact, it'll probably take you less time to make this shit than to order it, and it'll definitely taste better than whatever lukewarm crap comes to your door. So give the Postmates guy a fucking break. You can do this.

DF **Serves 2**

SUPER EASY STIR-FRY SAUCE
1/4 cup soy sauce

1/4 cup honey

2 cloves garlic

1 teaspoon minced ginger

1 tablespoon sesame seeds

OTHER TASTY SHIT
1 tablespoon olive oil

1 pound shrimp,
peeled and deveined

1/2 teaspoon salt

1/2 teaspoon pepper

Red pepper flakes (optional)

1 cup chopped broccoli

1 cup sliced red bell pepper

1/2 cup sliced red onion

1/2 cup sliced zucchini

1 Mix up all the sauce ingredients in a small bowl and set it aside.

2 Add the oil to a nonstick skillet over medium heat and let it warm up before dumping in the shrimp. Sprinkle in the salt, pepper, and red pepper flakes (if you want) and cook (and stir) the shrimp until they're opaque (cooked through), which should take 4-6 minutes.

3 Pour that delicious fucking stir-fry sauce over the shrimp and stir to coat them in it. Let the sauce start to simmer and bubble, then add the veggies to the pan and stir shit up again.

4 Cook everything for another few minutes until the veggies are tender-crisp, and you're done. Throw it over some leftover rice and enjoy while deleting all delivery apps from your phone. (Just kidding—that's just fucking crazy.)

Tasty Tip The sauce should thicken up a bit on its own, but you can always add a little cornstarch to help it along. Just mix 1 tablespoon cornstarch with 1 tablespoon water and whisk the mixture into your simmering stir-fry.

Creamy AF for VEGAN PASTA

Did you know that you can get all the delicious fucking creaminess of cream sauce without any actual cream? The combination of nut milk and nutritional yeast can do wonders to trick your taste buds into cheese-induced happiness. If you're not vegan and not so sure about eating yeast (enjoying that beer, BTW?), you can just swap the cashew milk for cow's milk and the nutritional yeast for lots of fucking Parm. Or give it a try as-is. You never know—this shit might just convert you.

DF | V | Veg
Serves 4-6

1 tablespoon olive oil

1 medium onion, diced

3 medium cloves garlic, minced

2 tablespoons tomato paste

1 pint grape tomatoes, halved

Salt and pepper

2½ cups vegetable broth

2½ cups cashew milk

16 ounces dried pasta

5 ounces fresh spinach

⅓ cup nutritional yeast

1 Grab a large pot or a Dutch oven—we're going to one-pot this bitch. Warm up the oil over medium heat, then add the onion and let it cook, stirring now and then, for 3-5 minutes until it's pretty translucent.

2 Stir in the garlic and tomato paste and let shit cook for another 3 minutes, stirring occasionally.

3 Stir in the tomatoes and cook everything for 3-5 minutes more, until the tomatoes start to wrinkle up (a.k.a. soften). Sprinkle in some salt and pepper, then stir in the broth, milk, and pasta. Bring things to a boil, then cover the pot, reduce the heat to low, and let shit simmer for 10 minutes so that the liquid gets absorbed.

4 Uncover the pot and stir in the spinach until it wilts. Then stir in the nutritional yeast until everything is creamy and you're ready to eat it right out of the fucking pot (which you totally can, if you want).

If you're not especially confident about cooking fish, you're not alone. But this choose-your-own-adventure-style recipe is not only versatile, it's also impossible to fuck up. Pick whatever skinless fish you like and follow a few easy steps to create the best fucking flaky, baked fish you and your lucky dinner guests have ever eaten.

Deliciously Fuck-Up-Free BAKED FISH

1 Get the broiler going on your oven and grease a 9 x 13-inch baking dish with the tablespoon of butter.

2 Toss everything but the fish into a small bowl and stir shit up.

3 Add the fish to your baking dish in a single layer, then put the whole thing in the oven to broil for 8 minutes.

4 Take the fish out of the oven, then spread your Parm mixture evenly over the fish. (Your fish should be flaky AF right now, so spread gently!)

5 Put the fish back in the oven to broil for another 2 minutes or so until everything is browned and bubbly. Then throw it over rice and veggies or a big-ass salad and prepare to savor the oohs and ahhs of your super-impressed family and friends (and some really good fucking fish).

GF **Serves 6**

1 tablespoon unsalted butter

$3/4$ cup shredded Parmesan

$1/3$ cup unsalted butter, softened

$1/4$ cup mayo

3 tablespoons lemon juice

$1/4$ cup chopped green onions

$1/4$ teaspoon salt

$1/4$ teaspoon black pepper

2 teaspoons dill weed

2 dashes Tabasco sauce

2 pounds skinless fish (tilapia, flounder, salmon—whatever you've got)

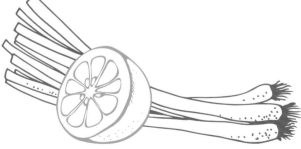

Fancy-Ass
Cheese-and-Pepper
PASTA
(A.K.A. CACIO E PEPE)

Not only is cacio e pepe hella easy to make, it's also been a go-to recipe for centuries. Really. This shit tracks back to Roman times. But that was pre-butter, and who wants to live in a pre-butter world? Not me! Today, this recipe is four ingredients' worth of fancy. So maybe act civilized and eat it at the dinner table instead of on the couch. (Yeah, who am I kidding?)

Serves 2

Salt, for pasta water

6 ounces dried spaghetti

3 tablespoons unsalted butter, cubed and divided

1 teaspoon black pepper

3/4 cup finely grated Grana Padano or Parmesan

1/3 cup finely grated Pecorino

1 Bring a large pot of water to a boil, throw in some salt and the spaghetti, and let the pasta cook (stirring now and then) for two minutes fewer than the box says to. (You're going to cook it a little more later.) When you drain the water off, keep 3/4 cup of it handy.

2 While the pasta cooks, start melting 2 tablespoons of the butter in a large skillet over medium heat. Stir in the pepper and then swirl it around like a fancy-ass chef for a minute until it toasts. (Did you know you could toast pepper? Yep. It's a thing.)

3 Add 1/2 cup of the reserved pasta water to the skillet and bring things to a simmer. Now stir in the pasta and the last tablespoon of butter. Reduce the heat to low and stir in the Grana Padano (tongs work well here) until it melts.

4 Take the skillet off the heat and stir in the Pecorino until it melts and everything looks all creamy and delicious. (If it's not saucy enough, stir in the last of the pasta water.) Then make sure you enjoy your pasta like a real Roman—with a never-empty glass of wine in hand.

Grown-Ass MAC 'N' CHEESE

You are a grown-ass adult with grown-ass taste buds. I don't want to see any fucking Easy Mac in that cupboard. Three cheeses, spices, browned-butter breadcrumbs—these are the hallmarks of real mac. And once you taste it, you'll never go back to that store-bought shit.

1 Bring a large pot of water to a boil and throw in some salt and a drizzle of oil (this already feels fancy, right?) Next, pour in the macaroni and let it cook as long as the box says it should, probably 6-8 minutes. Drain off all the water.

2 While that's going on: Preheat the oven to 350°F. Warm the milk in a small saucepan over low heat (don't let it boil). Grab a large pot for the actual making of the mac, melt the butter in it over low heat, and then whisk in the flour for a good 2 minutes. Continue whisking while you add the hot milk and cook the mixture for another minute or so until it's thick and smooth.

3 Take the pot off the heat (and turn off the damn burner), and stir in the cheeses, pepper, nutmeg, and then the pasta. Stir shit up until it's the kind of creamy mac you dream about.

4 Add the butter and panko breadcrumbs to the small saucepan over medium heat and stir them together until the butter has melted and been absorbed by the breadcrumbs. Let the breadcrumbs toast up a bit before taking them off the heat.

5 Pour your mac into an oven-safe skillet or baking dish, sprinkle the breadcrumbs over the top of it, pop it in the oven, and bake it for 10-15 minutes. Things should be bubbling and browned.

6 Finish things off with some fresh herbs, like cilantro or basil, and divide your grown-up mac between two grown-up bowls. Or eat it right out of the pan, because you're a grown-ass adult and you do what you want.

Tasty Tip Using Gruyère cheese makes this dish fair game for meat eaters, so why not throw some tasty fucking bacon or buffalo chicken into the mix?

Serves 4

Salt, for pasta water

1 tablespoon vegetable oil

2 cups elbow macaroni

1½ cups whole milk

2 tablespoons unsalted butter

2 tablespoons all-purpose flour

4 ounces Gruyère cheese, grated

3 ounces extra-sharp cheddar, grated

2 ounces bleu cheese, crumbled

¼ teaspoon pepper

1 pinch nutmeg

1 tablespoon unsalted butter

¼ cup panko breadcrumbs

Fresh herbs, for serving

Easy AF
CHICKEN MILANESE
WITH ARUGULA

I get it. You're ready to cook (and eat) like a fucking adult, but that doesn't mean you want to become Julia fucking Child. You just want some tasty shit that's easy to make and won't fuck with your bathroom scale. This. This is the recipe for you. Make it once and I guarantee it'll become your go-to meal.

GF **Serves 2-4**

2 large boneless, skinless chicken breasts

Salt and pepper

1/2 cup seasoned whole-wheat breadcrumbs

2 tablespoons grated Parmesan

1 large egg, beaten

1 teaspoon water

Olive oil spray

6 cups baby arugula

3 large lemons, cut into wedges

1 Preheat your oven to 425°F. Slice the chicken breasts into cutlets by taking a sharp knife horizontally through the chicken breasts from the thick end to the thin end. Place the cutlets between two sheets of plastic wrap and pound the crap out of them until they're an even 1/4-inch thick all around. Then sprinkle both sides with some salt and pepper.

2 Grab two shallow bowls. In one, whisk together the egg and teaspoon of water. In the other, combine the breadcrumbs and cheese.

3 Spray a foil-lined baking sheet with cooking spray (because washing two fucking dishes is enough). Dredge the chicken cutlets in the egg and then in the breadcrumbs, making sure they're well covered. Arrange them on the baking sheet, spray the tops of them with cooking spray, pop them in the oven, and bake them for 12-14 minutes, flipping them over halfway through the cook time.

4 Serve the baked cutlets on a bed of arugula with a spritz of lemon and some lemon wedges, like a fucking health-conscious adult.

I-Fucking-Love-Ranch
PORK CHOPS & VEGGIES

Cooking like a boss is super empowering, but it also takes a fucking eternity, and all that multitasking is hard. And then there's the fucking cleanup! But today, you're done with that bullshit. Armed with just a 3.5-ounce packet of the best fucking salad dressing (fight me), one pan, and about 30 minutes, you'll have a whole-ass meal that's ready to serve *at the same fucking time*. (FYI: you can swap out those green beans for whatever veggies or starches your little heart desires. Cherry tomatoes, Brussels sprouts, butternut squash—there isn't a single fucking thing that doesn't taste amazing when covered in ranch dressing mix and roasted in the oven.)

1 Preheat the oven to 425°F (that's set-off-the-fucking-smoke-detector hot, so be careful). In a small bowl, mix together the pork chop ingredients (except for the pork chops themselves, obvs) to create a delicious AF glaze.

2 Spray a large baking sheet with some olive oil spray. (Better yet, cover the pan with nonstick foil and avoid the miserable fucking cleanup entirely!) Slather the mixture over both sides of the pork chops, then place them in a row on one end of the baking sheet.

3 In a medium bowl, toss together all of the potato ingredients (that means stir shit up with a spatula). Pour the potatoes into a row next to the pork chops.

4 Bake the potatoes and pork chops for 15 minutes. While they're cooking, toss together the green bean ingredients in the same medium bowl you used for the potatoes (we're going for minimal cleanup here!).

5 At the 15-minute mark, remove the pan from the oven (and fan the smoke detector with a tea towel, if you have to). Use some tongs or a fork to flip the pork chops and pour the green beans into the remaining space in the pan. Return the pan to the oven and bake until the vegetables begin to brown, about 7 minutes.

6 Fancy that shit up with a sprinkle of parsley and serve it up to your super-impressed guests!

GF | DF Serves 4

RANCH PORK CHOPS

2 tablespoons honey

2 tablespoons Worcestershire sauce

2 tablespoons ranch dressing mix

2 tablespoons olive oil

2 tablespoons freshly chopped parsley

1 teaspoon minced garlic

1 teaspoon black pepper

1/2 teaspoon salt

4 boneless pork chops
(1/2 inch thick)

OMG-MORE-RANCH POTATOES

1 pound baby Yukon Gold potatoes, halved

1 tablespoon ranch dressing mix

2 tablespoons olive oil

1/4 teaspoon black pepper

1/4 teaspoon salt

YES-TO-ALL-THE-RANCH GREEN BEANS

8 ounces green beans, trimmed

1 tablespoon olive oil

Remaining ranch dressing mix

1/4 teaspoon black pepper

1/4 teaspoon salt

Up Your Fucking
RAMEN GAME

If you're still eating ramen out of a cup, it's time to get your shit together. Let's face it—your body had enough of that shit in college and your organs are probably still healing. This recipe uses the noodles you know and love (and that cost, like, 35 cents a pack) but offers some serious upgrades, like fresh fucking veggies.

VEG Serves 4

4 cups reduced-sodium vegetable broth

1 tablespoon sesame oil

3 medium cloves garlic, minced

2 teaspoons minced ginger

1 tablespoon soy sauce

1 tablespoon rice wine vinegar

1 large carrot, sliced

1 cup snow peas

1 large zucchini, sliced or spiralized

3 (3-ounce) packages ramen noodles

4 soft-boiled eggs

2 teaspoons sesame seeds

Drizzle sriracha (optional)

1 In a medium pot, combine the vegetable broth, sesame oil, garlic, ginger, soy sauce, and rice wine vinegar over medium heat. Let everything come to a boil, then reduce the heat and let it simmer for 7-10 minutes. (If you want to add some cooked veggies, like mushrooms or red peppers, now's the time to do it.)

2 Unpack the noodles, discard the seasoning packet, and toss the bricks into the pot. Let them cook for about 3 minutes, stirring now and then to break them up.

3 Time to dish it out! Top your ramen bowls with veggies, soft-boiled eggs, sesame seeds, and a drizzle of sriracha if you're feeling a little spicy.

I Make VEGGIE PAD THAI in My Damn Sleep

How fucking cool will you feel busting out some homemade Pad Thai for your friends? Who does that? You do that. Make sure you've got your ingredients at the ready, and then dazzle them with those badass culinary skills. (OK, a practice run couldn't hurt. But you got this!)

1 Grab a small bowl for the sauce ingredients, stir everything together, and set it aside.

2 Bring a large pot of water to a boil before throwing in the rice noodles. Let them cook for 1 minute, then take the pot off the burner and let them soak for another 5. Drain off the hot water, rinse the noodles with cold water, and move on to the tofu.

3 Add the vegetable oil to a large pan over medium-high heat. When it's warmed up, toss in the tofu and fry it until it's golden brown on all sides, then stir in the sesame seeds.

4 Add the noodles, sauce, veggies, and cilantro to the pan and stir shit up until the mushrooms soften up and everything heats through.

5 Serve up a heaping helping of this vegan excellence with a sprinkling of chopped peanuts and cilantro and a splash of lime juice.

Tasty Tip Get your shit together before you start a recipe and life will be infinitely easier. Slice up your veggies, boil anything that needs boiling, grab whatever baking crap you need. Just try to have everything ready to go so that you can focus on the actual fucking cooking.

GF | DF | V | VEG
Serves 4

YAY FOR GLUTEN-FREE SAUCE

4 tablespoons low-sodium tamari

2 tablespoons rice vinegar

4 tablespoons maple syrup

2 tablespoons lime juice

1 teaspoon sriracha

EVERYTHING ELSE

7 ounces stir-fry rice noodles

2-3 tablespoons vegetable oil

1 (16-ounce) block extra-firm tofu, cut into bite-size pieces

1 teaspoon sesame seeds

1 cup sliced mushrooms

4 baby bok choy

3 medium green onions, chopped

1/4 cup chopped cilantro, plus more for serving

2 medium limes, cut into wedges for serving

1/2 cup chopped peanuts, for serving

TEX-MEX FIESTA
in a Fucking
PEPPER

These scrumptious little self-contained burrito bowls are easy as fuck to make but taste like you slaved over a hot stove. Plus, anything served in a fucking vegetable is automatically impressive. Break these babies out when the in-laws visit and you might escape unscathed.

GF **Serves 6**

6 whole bell peppers
(dealer's choice on the color)

1/3 cup water

1 pound lean ground beef
(or turkey)

1 cup yellow onion, chopped

2 large garlic cloves, chopped

1 poblano pepper,
seeded and chopped

1 cup tomato puree or sauce

1 cup cooked rice or quinoa

1 cup fresh or thawed yellow corn

1 cup canned black beans,
drained and rinsed

2 tablespoons chili powder

2 teaspoons ground cumin

1 teaspoon salt

1/2 teaspoon pepper

1/2 cup grated Mexican-blend cheese

1 Preheat your oven to 350°F and prep the peppers: slice off the tops and remove the seeds and veins.

2 Set the peppers in a big baking dish and add 1/3 cup of water to the bottom of the dish. Cover the dish with some microwave-safe plastic wrap (or a couple of plates—whatever) and microwave the peppers on high for about 3 minutes so they soften up. Drain off the water, careful not to burn your fucking hands.

3 Grab a large skillet and cook the beef in it over medium-high heat. Once that's browned, drain off any fat (hands!) and stir in the onion, garlic, and poblano. Cook and stir everything until the onions are soft, then stir in the tomato puree, cooked rice, corn, beans, and spices. Then make sure you dig what you're making by trying a bite—now is the time to up the spice ante if you need to.

4 Spoon the beef mixture into the peppers waiting in the baking dish, then pop those babies in the oven for 25-30 minutes to let the peppers cook and the filling heat through.

5 Take out your baking dish, top the peppers with cheese, put the dish back in the oven for 5 minutes, and get excited for the delicious fucking fiesta you're about to throw for your mouth.

Have you ever wondered how steakhouses make those perfectly seared, super-fucking-flavorful steaks with almost no seasoning? It's the sear/bake combo, the timing of which depends on the cut of steak. For this one, we're creating mouthwatering filet mignon. (That's French for "really small fucking steak." It's small because it's the most decadent cut. But still, make sure you serve it with some hearty sides so you don't feel hosed.)

Now, That's a Fucking STEAK

1 Preheat the oven to 450°F and heat a cast-iron skillet over medium–high heat until it starts to smoke. (It's OK—it's supposed to do that.)

2 Sprinkle salt and pepper all over your steaks, using a little more than you think you should.

3 Throw the oil and butter into the skillet. Once the butter melts, place the steaks in the center of the skillet and don't fucking touch it for 3 minutes.

4 Use tongs to flip the steak and add the whole rosemary, thyme, and garlic to the pan.

5 Move the pan to the hot oven and let those bad boys cook for about 7 minutes for medium steaks.

6 Using the tongs, move the steaks to a cutting board and, again, don't fucking touch them for at least 5 minutes so the juices have a chance to settle in. Then serve up your perfect fucking filets with some fancy-ass wine.

GF **Serves 2**

Salt and pepper

1 tablespoon olive oil

2 tablespoons unsalted butter

2 (4-ounce) filet mignon steaks

2 sprigs fresh rosemary

1 sprig thyme

2 medium cloves garlic, peeled

1/2 teaspoon flaky sea salt (optional)

Tasty Tip Any nonstick skillet will do, but cast iron is fucking heaven-sent for searing steak.

Get Me a Fucking STEAK FAJITA STAT

Have you ever gone to a Mexican restaurant and watched jealously as the sizzling steak fajitas you did *not* think to order pass your fucking table? You never have to feel order remorse again, because you can just go home, throw some shit on a baking sheet, and whip up your own damn steak fajitas like you're making a PB&J. Only way more fucking satisfying.

1 Preheat your oven to 450°F and line a large baking sheet with nonstick foil ('cause fuck scrubbing).

2 Add the oil to a skillet over medium–high heat and let it heat up until it shimmers. Sear the steak for 2 minutes on each side (which means put it in the pan and don't fucking touch it for 2 minutes).

3 Drop the steak in the middle of the baking sheet, then surround it with the onions and peppers. Top everything with a drizzle of olive oil and sprinkle of spices (salt, pepper, chili, garlic, and cumin).

4 Get in there with your hands and rub all that good shit into the steak and veggies (all sides), then splash some lime over everything.

5 Pop the sheet into the oven and let it bake for 12 minutes (medium rare), or until the steak is how you like it.

6 Move the steak to a cutting board and let it rest for 10 minutes (seriously, don't fucking touch it) before slicing it into pieces against the grain.

7 Throw a little of everything into those warm tortillas, throw a little cilantro over top, and break out the good tequila to celebrate your awesome fucking cooking skills.

Tasty Tip If you like a little char on your fajita veggies, take just the steak out at the end of the cook time and let the veggies broil for a minute or two while the steak rests.

DF **Serves 4**

1 tablespoon olive oil
1 pound flank steak
1 medium green bell pepper, sliced
1 medium red bell pepper, sliced
½ medium red onion, sliced
Olive oil
Salt and pepper
Chili powder, to taste
Garlic powder, to taste
1 teaspoon cumin
Juice of ½ medium lime
8 flour tortillas, warmed
Fresh cilantro, for garnish

SHRIMP SCAMPI
with All the Good Shit

Wine and butter and garlic, OH MY! There's nothing to be afraid of in this quick dish—just all your favorite shit in every mouthwatering bite. And it's versatile as fuck. Serve this up as-is for a light lunch or throw it over veggies or gluten-free pasta for a decadent butter-infused dinner.

GF **Serves 4**

1¹/₂ pounds extra-large shrimp, peeled and deveined

2 medium green onions

¹/₃ cup clarified butter

4 tablespoons minced garlic

¹/₄ cup dry white wine

2 tablespoons fresh lemon juice

2 tablespoons freshly chopped parsley

Salt and pepper

Lemon wedges, for serving

1 Use a paper towel to pat the shrimp dry, then slice up the green onions (just the white/light green parts).

2 Melt the butter in a large skillet over medium heat, throw in the garlic, and stir it around for a minute or two until it softens up.

3 Throw the shrimp into the skillet along with the onions, wine, and lemon juice. Let the shrimp cook for 1-2 minutes per side until they're nice and pink. And don't overcook the damn things! No one likes tough shrimp.

4 Serve the shrimp up with a sprinkling of salt, pepper, and parsley and a wedge of lemon, then thank your lucky stars that you live in a universe with butter and garlic.

Tasty Tip Thinking *WTF is clarified butter?* I got you. Melt a stick of butter in a small saucepan (or microwave!) over low heat and let it simmer until it gets all foamy. When the butter stops bubbling, take it off the heat and skim off all the foam. To get it super smooth, run what's left through a strainer lined with cheesecloth. Voila! Clarified butter, the stuff of seafood dreams.

I Can't Even
LEMONY SALMON

When you have a night all to yourself and you're not about to people, you can go one of two routes: eat cereal right out of the fucking box or treat yourself to something good. This recipe has all the ease of the cereal box (I mean, basically), but it tastes like some serious self-care. So crack open the wine, cue up another episode of *The Great British Baking Show*, and congratulate yourself for making good choices. (Or at least starting to. I can't vouch for your dating life.)

GF | DF **Serves** 1

9 ounces trimmed asparagus

Olive oil

Salt and pepper

7 ounces skinless salmon

1 lemon wedge

3 slices white onion

2 slices lemon

1 sprig fresh dill

1 Preheat the oven to 350°F and lay out a 12 x 18-inch piece of parchment paper. Fold the paper in half, short end to short end, then back again. (I know, WTF. But you want the crease.)

2 Drop the asparagus on one side of the crease, drizzle some olive oil over it, then sprinkle it with salt and pepper, and toss it around a little to coat.

3 Place the salmon right on top of the veggies and top it off with a spritz of lemon plus a bit more oil, salt, and pepper.

4 Layer on the onion, lemon, and dill, then fold the paper over everything and seal that shit up (smoosh it along the edges).

5 Pop the pack onto a baking sheet and into the oven, then bake it for 20 minutes. (The internal temp of the salmon should be 145°F.) Once it's cooked, gently move it from the parchment to the elegant place setting you've set for yourself on the coffee table.

Super Fucking Posh
BUTTERNUT SQUASH & KALE
TORTE

"What the fuck is a torte?" you might find yourself wondering. Basically, it's a fancy-ass casserole. In fact, if you're not feeling that fancy (or don't have a fucking springform pan handy), just throw this shit into a casserole dish and call it a day. It'll taste fucking amazing no matter what it's baked in.

1 Preheat your oven to 425°F and grease a 9-inch springform pan with some cooking spray.

2 Cover the bottom of the pan with half the butternut squash (in concentric circles, if you're feeling especially elegant).

3 Layer on half of the onion rings, then half the kale, a drizzle of oil, some salt and pepper, all of the potato slices, and half the provolone.

4 Layer on the other half of the kale, the tomatoes, and the other half of the provolone. Top it off with the rest of the squash and the Parm.

5 Cover your tarte with foil, move it to a baking sheet, and pop it in the oven for 20 minutes. Then ditch the foil and bake it for another 8-10 minutes, or until the veggies are tender and starting to brown.

6 Serve up your fancy fucking torte to your fancy fucking guests and revel in your accomplishment, letting that one snide "You made this?" slide right off your back!

Serves 4

Cooking spray

½ small butternut squash, sliced into discs

1 medium red onion, cut into ¼-inch slices and rings separated.

1 small bunch kale

1 tablespoon olive oil

Salt and pepper

1 medium Yukon Gold potato, sliced into discs

6 ounces thinly sliced provolone

1 medium plum tomato, sliced

¼ cup grated Parmesan

Crusty bread, for serving

✳ Tasty Tip Quick reminder, most Italian cheeses are not full-on vegetarian. But you could totally sub in some cheddar or Swiss for the provolone and Parmesan here.

GRILL-MEETS-SOBA:
A Love Story

When you think of soup, you probably don't think of *grilled* veggies. But combine the two with Japanese soba noodles, and you get one hell of a refreshing, summery supper. And if you think it's good the first time around, try packing it for lunch and eating it cold. Talk about tasty as fuck!

1 Turn your grill (or your neighbor's grill—whatever) to medium heat and prep your eggplants: cut them into 1/4-inch-thick slices, sprinkle the slices with the salt, and arrange them between layers of paper towels to chill out for 15 minutes.

2 Lay out two 24-inch-long sheets of foil, stacked one on top of the other, and dump the beans on one half. Toss them with 2 teaspoons of sesame oil, then fold the doubled foil over them and crimp the edges to seal shit up.

3 Grill your bean packet for 16 minutes, turning it over once halfway through, and then set it aside.

4 Cook your noodles the way the box tells you to, then drain them, rinse them, and set them aside too.

5 Grab a large bowl and whisk together everything that's left (except the sesame seeds).

6 Using dry paper towels, press the last of the damn liquid out of the eggplant slices. Brush them each with some of the shit you just mixed up, then grill them with the cover on for 8-10 minutes, turning them over halfway through, until they're tender-crisp.

7 Toss everything into bowls, sprinkle some sesame seeds on top, and serve them up with a side of smug for being a multitasking master.

DF | VEG **Serves 4**

2 medium eggplants, Japanese ones if you've got 'em

1/2 teaspoon salt

8 ounces green beans

2 teaspoons toasted sesame oil

8 ounces soba noodles

3 tablespoons miso paste

2 tablespoons brown sugar

2 tablespoons red wine vinegar

1 tablespoon low-sodium soy sauce

2 medium cloves garlic, minced

2 teaspoons grated ginger

3 tablespoons toasted sesame oil

2 tablespoons water

Sesame seeds, for serving

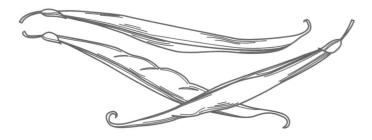

Idiot-Proof PESTO CHICKEN BAKE

This recipe is basic as fuck in the best possible way. Five ingredients (salt and pepper don't count—ask Rachel Ray), half an hour, and some parchment paper gets you a damn gourmet meal. All that's missing is a glass of wine, but I'm guessing you've got that shit handled too.

GF | DF **Serves 2**

2 boneless, skinless chicken breasts

10 ounces trimmed asparagus or broccoli florets

2 large Roma tomatoes, sliced

4 tablespoons pesto

2 tablespoons olive oil

Salt and pepper

1 Preheat the oven to 400°F and lay out two 12 x 18-inch pieces of parchment paper. Fold each paper in half, short end to short end, then back again to crease them.

2 Open each piece of parchment and divide the asparagus or broccoli between them, dropping them on one side of each crease. Throw some olive oil, salt, and pepper on the veggies and give them a quick toss to coat them.

3 Plop the chicken right on top of the veggies, sprinkle a little salt and pepper over top of it, spread some pesto on that shit, and top things off with the tomatoes.

4 For each packet, fold the parchment over and close it up by rolling the edges together like a really lazy piecrust.

5 Move your beautiful little bundles onto a baking sheet, throw it in the oven, and let things bake for 25-30 minutes. The internal temp of the chicken should be 165°F. (When it comes to chicken, it's better safe than sorry, so get a damn meat thermometer.)

6 Unwrap and enjoy this scrumptious gift from you to you. (How thoughtful of you!)

✱ Tasty Tip Need more servings? Make more packets. See how fucking easy that is?

Basically 4-Step
SEARED SCALLOP
RISOTTO

Super-indulgent seared-scallop risotto in just four steps? Yes, please! OK, so they're hearty steps. But this isn't complicated shit. Just sear, stir, and savor.

1 Whip up the risotto: Melt 1 tablespoon of the butter in a big nonstick skillet over medium heat, then throw in 1 minced clove of garlic and cook (and stir) it for a minute or two, until your house smells fucking amazing. Stir in the rice so that it gets all buttery, then pour in the wine. Stir in the broth $1/2$ cup at a time—simmer, stir, simmer, stir—until the rice is creamy (you don't have to use all of the broth). Finally, stir in the mushrooms, asparagus, Parm, and some salt and pepper.

2 Sear those fucking scallops: In another big nonstick skillet (or the same one washed out—whatever), warm up the grapeseed oil over medium-high heat. Wait for it to get nice and hot while you use paper towels to get the scallops totally dry, then sprinkle them with salt on all sides. Place the scallops in the pan in batches, making sure to give them some fucking breathing room, and then gently shake the pan to make sure they don't stick. When the bottoms start to brown (2-3 minutes), use tongs to flip each scallop over and cook them for another 30-90 seconds until they're firm and opaque. Move them to a paper towel-lined plate as they finish cooking.

3 Sauté the spinach, etc.: Wipe out the skillet (with plenty of paper towel between the hot surface and your fucking hand), then pour in the olive oil. Turn the heat to medium-low and stir in the remaining garlic for about a minute. Stir in the greens until they wilt.

4 Brown that butter: Add 3 tablespoons of butter to a small (totally different) skillet over medium heat and stir it continuously until it starts to look golden and foamy. Pour it into a heatproof bowl to cool down a bit, then drizzle it over each finished serving of scallop risotto for the most fucking indulgent thing you'll ever taste (next to, like, death-by-chocolate cake).

GF Serves 4

4 tablespoons unsalted butter, divided

2 cloves garlic, divided and minced

1 cup Arborio rice

$1/2$ cup white wine

3 cups chicken broth

5 ounces cooked and chopped wild mushrooms

7 ounces cooked and chopped asparagus

$1/2$ cup Parmesan

Salt and pepper

1 tablespoon grapeseed oil

1 pound sea scallops

1 tablespoon olive oil

4 cups baby spinach or kale

Chapter Four

HEALTHY SHIT
THAT TASTES UNHEALTHY

SPAGHETTI CARBONARA
for Skinny Bitches

What genius said, "Let's top some spaghetti with bacon, egg, and cheese?" They need a fucking award for creating this decadent dish. Bacon and cheese, sure. But who would have thought that a runny yolk could jazz up pasta? Amazing. Even smarter, though? This delicious, lightened-up version of the classic (designed to save us from ourselves).

1 Bring a large pot of salted water to a boil. Meanwhile, add the cold water, vinegar, and 1/4 teaspoon salt to a medium pot over high heat, bring it to a boil, and then drop it to low. (This is your egg-poaching liquid.)

2 Cook up your bacon in a deep skillet over medium-high heat until it starts to crisp up. Move the bacon to a paper towel-lined plate but leave the grease in the pan.

3 Drop your pasta into the boiling water and let it cook, stirring now and then, for 2 fewer minutes than the box tells you to. Then drain it, but don't rinse it.

4 While the pasta's cooking, add the broth to the bacon grease and let it simmer and reduce by a third, which should take 8-10 minutes. Then stir in the arugula, parsley, salt, and pepper, followed by the spaghetti. Bring the heat up to high and give the spaghetti a good fucking toss in the sauce to coat it.

5 Give the pasta another 2 minutes to cook, then remove the skillet from the heat, stir in the cheese, and give the spaghetti another toss.

6 Time to put that poaching liquid to good use. One at a time, crack an egg into a small bowl, then gently slide it into the simmering liquid. Let each egg cook until the white sets but the yolk is still runny, about 2-3 minutes. Use a slotted spoon to (really fucking carefully) get them out.

7 Divide the spaghetti among four bowls, top each off with its own fancy egg, some crumbled bacon, and black pepper.

8 If you go the egg route, break it open and stir the yolk into your creamy pasta while you quietly swear to yourself that the real diet starts tomorrow. Salads. Lots of salads.

Serves 4

Salt, for pasta water

4 cups cold water

6 tablespoons white vinegar

1/4 teaspoon salt

6 slices center-cut bacon

10 ounces dried spaghetti

3/4 cup low-sodium chicken broth

1 1/2 cups baby arugula, chopped

3 tablespoons
Italian parsley, chopped

1/4 teaspoon salt

Black pepper, to taste

1/4 cup grated Parmigiano-Reggiano cheese

3 tablespoons grated
Pecorino Romano

4 extra-large eggs

Find-Your-Fucking-Balance "GRAIN" BOWL

Your body wants this bowl. It needs this bowl. It's begging you for this bowl. You need vegetables to live, damn it! But you also need shit that tastes good, or what's the fucking point of living, amiright? Enter: this delightful concoction of roasted chickpeas, cauliflower rice, apples, and lime. It's called balance.

GF | DF | V | VEG
Serves 4

POWER SALAD MAKINGS

1 (14-ounce) can chickpeas, drained and rinsed

Olive oil

Chili powder, to taste

Salt and pepper

1 large head cauliflower, cut into florets

1 medium apple, thinly sliced

1 medium shallot, thinly sliced

1 handful parsley and mint, chopped

2 medium, firm avocados, diced

DRESSING IN A JAR

2 tablespoons grainy mustard

2 tablespoons honey

1/4 cup olive oil

1/4 cup water

Juice and zest of 1 lime

Salt and pepper

1 Preheat the oven to 400°F and line a baking sheet with parchment paper. Dump the chickpeas onto the baking sheet, drizzle them with olive oil, and sprinkle them with some chili powder, salt, and pepper (however much looks good to you). Pop these in the oven for 20-30 minutes, until they're nice and toasty.

2 Working in batches, toss the cauliflower into a food processor and pulse until you get something that resembles rice. (Don't go too fucking crazy or you'll end up with cauliflower puree.)

3 Throw all of the dressing ingredients into a Mason jar (or a storage container), pop on the top, and shake shit up. Then taste it and make adjustments if you need to.

4 Throw everything in a big-ass salad bowl, toss it together, and enjoy the sense of superiority that comes from eating healthy and actually fucking enjoying it!

Tasty Tip Parchment paper is super fucking handy to have around because it's nonstick and means the difference between scrubbing shit and not scrubbing shit, but foil works too. Just make sure it's the nonstick kind or it defeats the fucking point.

Fuck Fish Sticks, Make ROASTED TILAPIA & VEG

Time to ditch the fish sticks. This dish is just as easy as to make, but it's way fucking tastier. You roast the tomatoes, steam the beans, and bake the fish all on the same damn baking sheet, and in half an hour, you have a balanced meal you actually fucking *like*.

1 Preheat the oven to 500°F, then line a baking sheet with foil and give it a spritz with cooking spray. Add the tomatoes to the baking sheet, cut side up, and go over them with cooking spray and 1/4 teaspoon each of the salt and pepper. Then pop them in the oven for 5 minutes.

2 With the tomatoes still in the oven, drop the temp to 450°F. Pull out a large piece of foil, and drop the green beans onto one end of it. Top them with 1/4 teaspoon of the salt plus the oil and garlic, and use your hand to toss everything together. Fold the other half of the foil over the beans and seal shit up to make a packet, which you'll place on the baking sheet in the oven. (Just shove the fucking tomatoes over.) Bake everything for another 20 minutes.

3 Meanwhile, you're going to whip up a yummy moisture-trapping spread. Whisk together the mayo, juice, tarragon, and Dijon in a small bowl. Sprinkle your fish all over with the last 1/4 teaspoon each of the salt and pepper, then spread the mayo mix over the top of each fillet. Top everything with panko and a spritz of cooking spray (which will help crisp shit up).

4 Take the baking sheet out of the oven, make room on it for the fish fillets, and pop it back in the oven for about 6 minutes. Then turn the oven up to broil and let that shit cook for another 3 minutes until you have golden, flaky deliciousness in fish form. Serve everything up with lemon wedges and say goodbye to fish sticks, because you're fucking better than that now.

Serves 4

Cooking spray

4 medium plum tomatoes, halved lengthwise

3/4 teaspoon salt, divided

1/2 teaspoon black pepper, divided

12 ounces green beans, trimmed

1 tablespoon olive oil

2 medium cloves garlic, thinly sliced

1/4 cup canola mayo

2 teaspoons fresh lemon juice

1 1/2 teaspoons freshly chopped tarragon

1 teaspoon Dijon mustard

4 (6-ounce) tilapia fillets

1/3 cup panko breadcrumbs

8 lemon wedges, for serving

Lighten the Fuck Up
CAULIFLOWER-CRUST
PIZZA

Cauliflower-crust pizza is proof that eating healthy doesn't have to be so fucking serious. You are allowed to watch what you eat and enjoy the hell out of your food! Not only does this crust help you ditch that heavy I-ate-too-much-fucking-pizza feeling, it also sneaks in whole servings of veggies. And sneaky veggies really are the best kind.

GF | VEG *Serves* **2-4**

1 head cauliflower, stalk removed

1/2 cup shredded mozzarella

1/4 cup grated Parmesan

1/2 teaspoon dried oregano

1/2 teaspoon salt

1/4 teaspoon garlic powder

2 large eggs, lightly beaten

Whatever the hell you want on your pizza

1 Preheat the oven to 400°F and line a baking sheet with parchment paper. Break up the cauliflower into florets (or just take out some anger and rip it apart—it's getting ground the fuck up anyway) and pulse it into cauliflower dust in a food processor a handful at a time.

2 Pour the cauliflower into a microwavable bowl, cover it up, and pop it in the microwave for 4-6 minutes to soften up. Dump it out onto a clean, dry kitchen towel and let it cool before you wring it out. (You want to get all the moisture out without burning your fucking hands.)

3 Throw all of the ingredients into a big bowl and stir shit up.

4 Grab a baking sheet or a pizza stone and spread the mix into a circle or, you know, a pizza crust.

5 Pop your pizza crust in the oven and bake it for 20 minutes, then throw whatever the hell you want on top of it and bake it for 10 more minutes. Give your muse free rein! (Except if you're one of those pineapple and ham people—keep that shit locked down.)

---

*Tasty Tip Let's get fucking real: cauliflower crust is super yummy, but it's never going to be pizza dough. Lean into the difference by getting inventive with your topping combos—think chicken alfredo or balsamic tomato instead of classic margherita.

Refreshing AF
THREE-CITRUS SALMON SALAD

Listen, you can't live on salad alone. A few days of mixed greens and cucumbers will have you hitting the drive-thru in no time. If you're going to have a salad for dinner, have a fucking *salad*. Broiled salmon, avocado, citrusy vinaigrette—this shit is a complete meal in a bowl. You'll never look at salad the same way again.

1 Line a baking sheet with nonstick foil and set the salmon fillets on it.

2 Divide 2 teaspoons of the Dijon, 1/2 teaspoon of the dried parsley, 1/4 teaspoon of the salt, and however much black pepper you want among the 4 fillets.

3 Turn the oven to broil and move the rack to the top position. Broil the salmon for 6-7 minutes until it's cooked through and flaky.

4 Grab a large bowl and whisk together all of the vinaigrette ingredients, then set it aside while you get the rest of your shit together.

5 Divide all of the salad makings among four bowls (or plates, or parfait glasses for all I care), top with those perfect little cuts of salmon, and top everything off with a drizzle of homemade blood-orange dressing because you are basically Martha fucking Stewart right now. Except without the weed. (Or maybe not?)

GF | DF Serves 4

AMPED UP SALMON

4 (4-ounce) salmon fillets

2 teaspoons Dijon mustard

1/2 teaspoon dried parsley

1/4 teaspoon salt

Black pepper, to taste

BAD-ASS BLOOD ORANGE VINAIGRETTE

1/2 teaspoon fine blood orange zest

3/4 cup freshly squeezed blood orange juice

2 tablespoons freshly squeezed lemon juice

2 tablespoons whole-grain mustard

1 teaspoon salt

1/2 teaspoon black pepper

3/4 cup vegetable oil

FANCY FIXINS

2 small avocados, sliced

4 cups mixed greens

1 blood orange, halved and sliced

1 tablespoon sunflower seeds

1 lime, sliced into wedges, for serving

All-Fucking-Powerful
FARRO BOWL

Feel like you're riding the struggle bus lately? This ancient-grain bowl is packed with protein and brain-boosting ingredients, which is exactly what you need to power the fuck up and get your shit together. And it's way more fucking satisfying than an energy drink. Plus, the more often you eat like this, the better you'll feel. (The same definitely cannot be said for energy drinks.)

DF | V | VEG Serves 4

1 cup whole-grain farro

2 cups low-sodium vegetable broth

1½ teaspoons salt

1 dried bay leaf

1 large shallot, thinly sliced

1 tablespoon vegetable oil

More salt

⅓ cup extra-virgin olive oil

3 tablespoons apple cider vinegar

1 tablespoon Dijon mustard

2 teaspoons honey

Black pepper, to taste

2 cups lightly packed arugula

1 medium green apple, chopped

½ cup feta cheese

¼ cup freshly chopped basil

⅛ cup freshly chopped parsley

¼ cup toasted pecans, roughly chopped

1 First up: cook the farro. (You might want to put on a podcast for this part.) Grab a medium saucepan and add the farro, broth, salt, and bay leaf to it. Bring it to a boil over high heat, then reduce it to low heat to simmer. Let it cook, stirring now and then, until the broth is gone and the farro is tender, about 30 minutes. Move it to a large bowl to cool down while you do other shit.

2 Throw the shallots and vegetable oil into a small saucepan over medium heat. When the shallots start to bubble, reduce the heat to medium-low and let them cook (stirring now and then) for 15-20 minutes, until they're crispy and golden. Then use a slotted spoon to move them to a paper towel-lined plate. Sprinkle a little salt over them and let them cool.

3 Next, whip up the dressing: stir together the olive oil, vinegar, mustard, honey, and some salt and pepper in a medium bowl.

4 Finally, put all that good shit together with all the other shit that's on the list. I don't have to tell you how to make a fucking grain bowl, right? Just throw everything in a bowl and dig in!

Let's be honest, here. You're not going to be tricked into thinking that zucchini noodles are spaghetti. But you can get behind some teriyaki-soaked veggies, right? This chicken stir-fry is the way zoodles were meant to be eaten—you know, like a fun take on a delicious fucking vegetable and not a pasta noodle, which they definitely are not.

The Best Fucking Use of ZOODLES
(WITH TERIYAKI CHICKEN)

DF Serves 4

1 Warm the oil up in a large pan over medium-high heat while you prep the chicken: sprinkle salt and pepper over both sides, then cut it into 1-inch pieces.

2 Add the chicken to the skillet and let it cook for 3-4 minutes on each side (go easy on the stirring—give it a damn chance to brown) until it's cooked through and sporting some lovely color.

3 Throw the peppers into the pan and let everything cook for another 3-5 minutes, until the peppers have softened. Then stir in the garlic and ginger for another 30 seconds.

4 While you're patiently waiting for the chicken and peppers to cook (and not fucking disturbing them), prep the sauce: Add the soy sauce, water, brown sugar, honey, and sesame oil to a small pot over medium-high heat and stir until the sugar dissolves, about 3 minutes. Crank the heat up to high and bring that delicious shit to a boil. In a little bowl, stir the cornstarch into the cold water until it dissolves, then stir the slurry (that's legit what it's called) into the sauce and let it boil and thicken up for 1-2 minutes.

5 When the peppers have softened, add the zoodles to the pan and let shit cook for another 3-4 minutes so that they soften up. Finally, pour that scrumptious stir-fry sauce over everything, top things off with some sesame seeds, and listen for the faint cries of the Chinese-food restaurant that is losing your business as you chew.

1¼ pounds boneless, skinless chicken breasts

2 teaspoons vegetable oil

1 cup chopped bell peppers

2 teaspoons minced garlic

2 teaspoons minced ginger

¼ cup low-sodium soy sauce

½ cup water

3 tablespoons brown sugar

1 tablespoon honey

1 teaspoon toasted sesame oil

1 tablespoon cornstarch

2 tablespoons cold water

3 medium zucchinis, spiralized into noodles

1 tablespoon sesame seeds

Salt and pepper

Tasty Tip Don't feel like spiralizing some noodles? Didn't even know that was a thing? I'm not going to make you work for it. Just grab some from the veggie section.

Worship-Worthy
GREEN GODDESS COBB

This scrumptious salad is what leftovers should fucking aspire to be—healthy, delicious, filling, and smile-inducing. Oh, and it's easy as hell to pull together. (OK, yeah, if you don't have leftovers, you'll have to grill some chicken, hard-boil some eggs, and cook some bacon. Otherwise, it's super chill.)

1 Literally just throw all of the salad ingredients into a large bowl—I genuinely don't care how. If you want it to look pretty, make sure it looks pretty. But it's going to taste fucking amazing no matter how it looks!

2 Throw all of the dressing ingredients into a blender or a food processor and blend them up for 30-45 seconds until you have the smooth and creamy green goddess dressing of your dreams. Drizzle (or pour) that shit over your immaculately arranged salad, and say your thanks to the goddess of delicious fucking greens.

Tasty Tip Green goddess dressing is not some delicate little vinaigrette. It's more like a Caesar. Drizzle it onto your salad, but then make sure you stir shit up really well to coat your greens and get that amazing fucking flavor in every bite.

WHAT I CALL
A FUCKING SALAD

6 ounces mixed greens

6 ounces grilled chicken breast, sliced

2 tablespoons crisply cooked bacon crumbles

3 tablespoons diced avocado

$1/2$ cup sliced red onion

2 large hard-boiled eggs, sliced in half

2 tablespoons feta cheese

DROOL-INDUCING DRESSING

1 cup mayo

2 tablespoons tarragon leaves

3 tablespoons minced chives

1 cup fresh flat leaf parsley

1 cup packed watercress, cleaned and tough stems removed

2 tablespoons lemon juice

1 tablespoon champagne vinegar

$1/2$ teaspoon salt

$1/4$ teaspoon pepper

A CHICKEN BURRITO BOWL
in Salad's Clothing

This isn't a salad. It may look like a salad, but it's not a salad. This is a burrito bowl with extra lettuce. OK, yeah, it's a salad. But it's a really fucking good one. And I'm not even going to make you go cold-turkey on the carbs! Just add some damn rice if you can't live without it. Either way, you'll enjoy every delicious fucking bite of this non-salad salad.

1 Drop the chicken and all of its seasoning ingredients into a big zip-top bag, seal it up, and shake it around. (Kind of cathartic, right?) Let it marinate for at least 10 minutes, but that shit can sit in your fridge for up to 2 days if you want it to.

2 When the chicken's all set, add some oil to a heavy skillet over medium-high heat and let it get nice and hot. Then place the chicken in the skillet and let it cook for 4-5 minutes on each side. (Don't fucking manhandle it, either. Aim to flip it just the once.) Take the skillet off the heat and let the chicken rest for 5 minutes before you slice it up for your salad.

3 Throw all of those beautiful fucking salad ingredients into a big bowl, then whip up some creamy cilantro-lime goodness (i.e., add the dressing ingredients to a food processor and pulse them together for a few seconds). Drizzle the dressing over the salad and try not to think about how much money you've wasted on burrito bowls that don't taste nearly as good as this fucking salad.

BLAND CHICKEN CAN FUCK OFF

2 boneless, skinless chicken thighs

1 tablespoon taco seasoning

$1/2$ teaspoon cumin

$1/4$ teaspoon salt

Juice of $1/2$ medium lime

1 tablespoon olive oil

BURRITO SALAD INGREDIENTS

2 cups romaine lettuce, chopped

1 medium avocado, sliced

1 medium tomato, diced

$1/2$ cup canned kidney or black beans, drained and rinsed

$1/2$ cup canned corn, drained and rinsed

$1/4$ cup cooked white rice (optional)

$1/4$ cup cilantro, for serving

$1/4$ cup shredded Mexican blend cheese, for serving

I-HEART-CILANTRO-LIME DRESSING

$1/2$ cup sour cream or Greek yogurt

$1/4$ cup packed cilantro with stems

Juice of $1/2$ medium lime

$1/4$ teaspoon salt

Cauliflower "MAC" ATTACK

Subbing in cauliflower for noodles in your mac 'n' cheese may sound extreme, but it's really just one of the best fucking ways to eat cauliflower. Here's the key: don't skimp on the fucking cheese. Keep it fresh, and none of that nonfat shit. You're already going healthy; you don't need to be a fucking martyr. Just lose the carbs and keep the flavor.

VEG Serves 6

$1^1/_2$ teaspoons salt, divided

8 cups chopped cauliflower florets ($^1/_2$-inch pieces)

1 tablespoon unsalted butter

2 teaspoons olive oil

$^1/_4$ cup minced onion

3 tablespoon all-purpose flour

2 cups fat-free milk

Black pepper, to taste

2 cups shredded sharp cheddar

1 Preheat your oven to 400°F. Add an inch of water to a large pot, then add 1 teaspoon of salt and bring the water to a boil over medium-high heat. Toss in the cauliflower and let it cook until it's tender-crisp (so, 6-7 minutes). Drain off the water and throw the cooked cauliflower in a bowl for now.

2 Add the butter and oil to a large saucepan over medium heat and let the butter melt. Then add the onions and cook (and stir) them for about 2 minutes so they soften up. Stir in the flour, then reduce the heat to low, grab a whisk, and exercise that fucking wrist for another 3-4 minutes.

3 Pour in the milk while you whisk, then bring the heat up to medium-high and let it come to a boil while you whisk for another couple of minutes (your wrist will be hella strong after this). That shit should be thick and creamy. When it is, whisk in $^1/_2$ teaspoon of salt and some pepper, then move the pan off the heat entirely (and turn off the burner, obvs).

4 Let the mixture stop boiling before you start stirring in the cheese $^1/_4$ cup at a time, making sure it melts into the sauce before you add more. Just keep stirring (sing it like Dory if you have to).

5 Stir in the cooked cauliflower until it's all cheesed up, then pour everything into a baking dish. Pop that in the oven and let it bake for 15-20 minutes until it's golden and bubbly, then turn the temp up to broil and let the top brown for another couple of minutes. Finally, divide it into bowls and watch your kids devour that shit like it's bad for them!

When's the last time you heard someone call tequila healthy? Never, because it's not. (Sorry!) But since the alcohol burns off, you get all the flavor of your favorite adult beverage and none of the guilt/hangover/bad decisions. Plus, you save calories for other fun things. I'm not going to say "margaritas," but...

TEQUILA-LIME
CHICKEN
(Shots Optional)

GF **Serves 4**

3 tablespoons olive oil

3 tablespoons tequila

1 tablespoon lime zest

4 cloves garlic, minced

1$\frac{1}{4}$ teaspoons ground ancho chili pepper

$\frac{1}{2}$ teaspoon ground coriander

$\frac{1}{4}$ teaspoon dried oregano

1$\frac{1}{4}$ teaspoons salt

$\frac{1}{2}$ teaspoon black pepper

2 teaspoons honey

4 boneless, skinless chicken thighs

Olive oil, for cooking

1 medium lime, sliced into wedges, for serving

1 Literally throw everything, up to (but not including) the chicken, into a 1-gallon zip-top freezer bag, zip the bag, and squish it like Silly Putty until it resembles a marinade.

2 Place the chicken between two pieces of plastic wrap (so you don't have to bleach your countertops, though it's never a bad idea), and pound the crap out of it until it's all an even $\frac{1}{2}$-inch thick.

3 Add the chicken to the bag, close it, and toss it around. Then set it in a bowl or a baking dish ('cause leaks happen), pop it in the fridge, and let it marinate overnight.

4 Warm up a little olive oil in a nonstick skillet over medium-high heat.

5 Cooking in batches of two, place the chicken thighs in the pan and spoon some extra marinade over them. Ditch whatever's left, then cook the chicken for 5-7 minutes per side until it's cooked through and reaches an internal temp of 165°F. (Don't manhandle the damn things—just turn them once.)

6 Serve them up with a splash of lime, some rice, and an ice-cold margarita. You know, for authenticity.

Tasty Tip You can't crowd the chicken or it won't cook properly, but there's no rule against having two skillets going at once so that everything's done at the same fucking time!

BUTTERNUT SQUASH PILAF
(a.k.a. Vegan Comfort Food)

What do vegans do when life gets hard and they can't drown their sorrows in cheese or ice cream? They curl up with the latest Michael Pollan book and a warm, hearty bowl of this little beauty, which offers up the calming effects of rice, wine, and creamy winter squash. In fact, this might even be better than cheese. You should try it and find out.

DF | GF | V | VEG
Serves 4

2 tablespoons olive oil

1 small yellow onion, diced

2 medium cloves garlic, minced

1 teaspoon fresh thyme

1½ cups Arborio rice

1 teaspoon salt

Black pepper, to taste

½ cup dry white wine

4 cups butternut squash, cubed

4 cups vegetable broth

Fresh parsley, for garnish

1 Preheat your oven to 375°F. Warm up the olive oil in a large Dutch oven over medium heat, then add the onions and cook (and stir) them for 3-4 minutes. Add the garlic and keep stirring for another couple of minutes until your kitchen starts to smell like a good Italian restaurant. Then stir in the thyme and cook everything for another 2 minutes.

2 Add the rice to the pot and sauté it until it's lightly toasted, then stir in the salt, pepper, and white wine. Now stir in the squash and vegetable broth, turn up the heat, and bring everything to a boil.

3 Cover the pot, pop it in the oven, and let it bake for 15-20 minutes. Once all the liquid is absorbed, divide it into bowls with a little fresh parsley sprinkled over top. Or eat it straight out of the fucking pot. Whatever. No judgment when it tastes this good.

Tasty Tip Have you ever tried to chip away at a raw butternut squash? It's an exercise in futility. Instead, cut off both ends of the squash, use a fork to poke holes all over it, and microwave it on high for 3-4 minutes. Then you can peel off the skin and chop that sucker up no problem. (Or just buy frozen squash. Really depends on your level of commitment.)

BIG-ASS BUDDHA BOWL
with Spicy Chickpeas

I'll let you in on a little secret: you don't have to fucking suffer for the sake of your health. If you're used to eating food that tastes like cardboard, that shit ends now. This buddha bowl is both healthy as fuck *and* overflowing with flavor. It's got creamy, crunchy, heat, sweetness, and a little mouth-puckering tartness for good fucking measure. If that's not a recipe for health-food happiness, I don't know what the hell is.

1 Toss the chickpeas, salt, pepper, chili powder, and garlic powder into a good-size bowl, and stir shit up until the chickpeas have a good coating.

2 Let a skillet heat up over medium heat, then pour in the chickpeas and let them cook for 10 minutes, stirring them every so often, until they're good and toasty. (Skip the Bobby Flay-style skillet toss, show-off. A fucking spatula will do.)

3 While your chickpeas cook, add all of the dressing ingredients to a food processor or high-speed blender and blend that shit up until it's smooth and creamy. Set that aside for now.

4 Divide the quinoa and all of the veggies between two big-ass bowls, and top things off with the sliced avocado, some lime juice, and a heavy-handed drizzle of delicious fucking lime dressing. Then bask in the glow of your healthy choices!

Tasty Tip Want to up that flavor ante? Throw the sliced red pepper and Brussels sprouts onto a baking sheet with some olive oil, salt, and pepper. Get in there with your hands and stir shit up so that the veggies are coated, slip the baking sheet into an oven preheated to 400°F, and let them roast for 15 minutes before adding them to your bowl.

DF | V | VEG Serves 2

THAT BIG-ASS BUDDHA BOWL

1 cup chickpeas, drained

1/2 teaspoon salt,
plus more to taste

1/2 teaspoon freshly ground pepper,
plus more to taste

1 teaspoon chili powder

1 teaspoon garlic powder

1 1/2 cups cooked quinoa

1 cup spinach (or whatever
fucking leafy green you've got)

1/4 cup red cabbage

1 medium red bell pepper, sliced

1 handful large Brussels sprouts,
sliced if you want

1 large avocado, sliced

Juice of 1 lime

FUCKING PERFECTION
IN A VEGAN DRESSING

1/2 large avocado

3 tablespoons lime juice

3/4 cup water

1 tablespoon olive oil

1 cup chopped fresh cilantro,
loosely packed

1 clove garlic, minced

1 teaspoon maple syrup

1/2 teaspoon fine sea salt

Black pepper, to taste

SWEET POTATO QUINOA BOWL

Is Basically a Damn Vitamin

Quinoa, sweet potatoes, spinach, avocado, olive oil—the number of superfoods in this grain bowl is fucking ridiculous. And so is the fact that they're tasty as fuck when combined. What are the odds of that? This is one big bowl of absurdly healthy, stupidly delicious shit that you get to feel really fucking good about making.

DF | V | VEG **Serves 2**

1½ cups cooked quinoa

1 tablespoon olive oil

1-2 sweet potatoes, chopped

3 cups spinach or kale

1 medium avocado, diced

3 tablespoons olive oil

1 tablespoon fresh lemon juice

1 pinch of black pepper

¼ -½ teaspoon chili powder (optional)

¼ teaspoon onion powder (optional)

1 Add the olive oil to a large skillet over medium–high heat and let it warm up before you throw the potatoes on top of it. Let them cook, stirring now and then, until you have a hard time not putting one in your mouth because they're soft and browned (about 30 minutes).

2 If you're using leftover quinoa, warm it up in a small saucepan over medium heat. Then stir in your greens, pop the top on, and give it about 3 minutes for the greens to wilt. (If you like the crunch of fresh greens, ditch this step and just throw them on top your finished bowls.)

3 Divide the quinoa and potatoes between two bowls—or throw it in one big bowl, depending on how fucking hungry you are—and top things off with some fresh avocado.

4 Stir up the remaining ingredients in a small bowl, drizzle that shit all over your sweet-potato quinoa, and get ready to power up like a Super Mario Bros. character.

Tasty Tip Half an hour is a long fucking time to cook potatoes. Make life easier by wrapping the potatoes in a damp paper towel, microwaving them for a few minutes, and then frying them. You'll cut the cooking time in half and end up with potatoes that are deliciously fucking crispy outside and soft inside.

CHEESY BROCCOLI CHICKEN BAKE
Glow Up

This isn't some unloved little Velveeta-slathered broccoli-chicken casserole. This bake is post-divorce and has taken some "me time" to rediscover itself. It's added a little quinoa to the mix, some Gruyère, and a few fiery spices, and it's ready to take center fucking stage on your dinner table.

Serves 4

Cooking spray

2 tablespoons olive oil

2 tablespoons all-purpose flour

1 cup whole milk

1 cup reduced-sodium chicken broth

2 pounds boneless, skinless chicken breasts

1/2 teaspoon salt

1/2 teaspoon poultry seasoning

1 dash paprika

1 dash cayenne pepper

1 cup uncooked quinoa, rinsed

1/2 cup cooked, crumbled bacon

Salt, for boiling water

3 cups fresh broccoli florets

1 cup shredded Gruyère cheese

1 Preheat the oven to 400°F and coat a square baking dish with a good layer of cooking spray.

2 Whip up that creamy sauce: Grab a medium skillet and warm up the olive oil in it over medium-high heat. Add the flour and then get to whisking until everything gets all bubbly, golden, and toasted. Work those fucking wrist muscles as you whisk in the milk and chicken broth until the sauce gets foamy and creamy, then take it off the heat.

3 Set the chicken breasts on a cutting board and sprinkle them all over with the salt, poultry seasoning, paprika, and cayenne. Then cut them up into 1/4-inch pieces.

4 Grab your casserole dish and throw in the rinsed quinoa, sauce, and bacon. Top things off with the chicken before putting the dish in the oven and letting it bake, uncovered, for 45 minutes. (You want the quinoa to absorb all of the liquid.)

5 While the chicken bakes, blanch your broccoli (which is fancy-chef-talk for boiling it and then throwing it in ice water so that it stops cooking): Bring a large pot of salted water to a boil, toss in the broccoli, and let it cook for 1 minute until it's bright green. Pour the pot out over a fine-mesh sieve (or colander-whatever the hell you have handy), then drop the sieve into a bowl/pot of ice water. Shake off the excess water and let the broccoli chill (literally) until your 45 minutes are up.

6 After 45 minutes, the casserole base should be cooked through. Layer on the broccoli and cheese, pop the whole thing back in the oven to bake for another 5 minutes, then crank up the heat to broil and let that shit brown to golden, cheesy perfection.

OMFG
CHICKEN
& ZUCCHINI

So, you want a recipe that's tasty as fuck, easy as hell to make, and not going to fuck with your diet? You know what? Sounds completely fucking reasonable to me. This crave-worthy Parmesan-crusted chicken and zucchini checks all the boxes and tastes like a sign from on high that your standards are right where they fucking should be.

1 Preheat your oven to 425°F and cover two baking sheets with nonstick foil. (Oh, and make sure you have room for two baking sheets in your oven before you turn the fucking thing on. That's helpful.)

2 For the chicken: Lay the chicken on one baking sheet. Mix up the mayo and Parm for the chicken and spread it evenly over the chicken thighs , then sprinkle everything with the breadcrumbs. Pop that into the oven to cook for 20 minutes. (Seriously, that's it.)

3 For the zucchini: Lay the zucchini on the other baking sheet and drizzle it with olive oil. Mix up the Parm, thyme, oregano, basil, and garlic in a bowl, then sprinkle it over the zucchini. Pop the zucchini into the oven about 8 minutes into your chicken's cook time.

4 When your 20-minute timer goes off, take the chicken out and let it rest while you move your zucchini up to the top rack, set the oven to broil, and let the veggies brown for 2-3 minutes under your watchful gaze.

5 Plate it all up, sprinkle it with parsley, and get ready to crave this shit at least once a week from now on.

Tasty Tip Your smoke detector is not a fucking kitchen timer. Pause long enough to ask Alexa to set a timer so you don't fuck up your amazing food.

Serves 4

JUICY CHICKEN DELICIOUSNESS

1/2 cup olive-oil mayo

1/4 cup grated Parmesan

4 boneless, skinless chicken thighs (about 1 1/4 pounds)

4 teaspoons Italian breadcrumbs

INSANELY GOOD ZUCCHINI

4 zucchinis, quartered lengthwise to create spears

2 tablespoons olive oil

1/2 cup freshly grated Parmesan

1/2 teaspoon dried thyme

1/2 teaspoon dried oregano

1/2 teaspoon dried basil

1/4 teaspoon garlic powder

Salt and pepper

2 tablespoon chopped fresh parsley leaves, for serving

Sweet as Fucking Honey
SALMON & BROCCOLI

Just you tonight? Sure, you could hit the drive-thru on your way home. Or you could treat yourself to a whole-ass meal that actually fucking tastes good. Did I mention it takes, like, two minutes of your time to throw together? Yeah. Choose this. Those fries will be cold by the time you get home anyway.

DF **Serves 1**

6 ounces skinless salmon

1 teaspoon minced garlic

1 teaspoon minced ginger

1/4 teaspoon black pepper

2 tablespoons soy sauce (or tamari)

1 tablespoon honey

1 cup broccoli florets

1/2 cup sliced mushrooms

1/2 cup green beans

Olive oil

Salt and pepper

1 teaspoon sesame seeds, for serving

1/2 medium avocado, sliced for serving

1 soft-boiled egg (optional)

1 Preheat your oven to 400°F and line a baking sheet with some parchment paper.

2 Lay the salmon on one side of the baking sheet. In a small bowl, stir together the garlic, ginger, black pepper, soy sauce, and honey to make a sticky, sweet glaze for your salmon.

3 Pour the glaze over the salmon, then flip the fish so that it's saucy on both sides.

4 Lay the veggies on the other side of the baking sheet. Drizzle some olive oil over them, followed by a sprinkling of salt and pepper, then use your hands to toss the veggies and make sure they're good and seasoned.

5 Pop the whole thing into the oven and let it bake for 10-12 minutes until the salmon is perfectly cooked and flaky and the veggies are tender. Sprinkle the sesame seeds over your creation and plate with the avocado and the soft-boiled egg if you please. Then take your super healthy plate of honey-soy deliciousness into the living room and eat it in front of the TV, like a normal person. (It's called *balance*.)

Tasty Tip You can whip up that sticky sauce about an hour before you're ready to eat and let the salmon marinate in it for a stronger flavor. And switching to tamari instead of soy makes the whole damn thing gluten free!

Tasty AF
TURKEY BURGER

As much as fitness bloggers want you to think so, a turkey burger is not the fucking same as a beef burger. A turkey burger is its own incredible creation, so you have to play to its strengths with things like sweet-tart cranberry sauce and fresh herbs. Sure, caramelizing the onions takes a minute, but it's so fucking worth it.

1 Throw the cranberries, sugar, and orange juice (or water, if you're allergic to flavor) into a small saucepan over medium heat and bring things to a boil. Then reduce the heat and let shit simmer for 10-12 minutes, stirring now and then, before taking it off the heat and setting it aside.

2 Next up, caramelize the onions: Warm up the olive oil in a large sauté pan over medium-high heat, then toss in the onion slices and sprinkle them with $1/2$ teaspoon of salt. Start cooking and stirring until the onions get soft, then juicy, and finally start to brown. (And OMFG...that intoxicating smell.) Add a little water to the pan in the last five minutes to release those yummy stuck-on bits, then keep stirring until the onions are browned to sweet perfection. Set these aside while you whip up your turkey burgers.

3 Grab a large bowl and toss in the breadcrumbs, parsley, sage, pepper, turkey, and the last $1/4$ teaspoon of salt. Stir shit up so that it's fully combined, then divide the mix into 4 patties. Press your thumb into the center of the patties to make a deep indentation (sounds weird, but this will actually make the burger end up even instead of puffing up like a prep-school football star).

4 Warm up a grill pan over medium-high heat, give it a spritz with cooking spray, and add the patties to the pan. Grill them for 5 minutes, then flip them and let them cook for another 3 minutes. Sprinkle however fucking much cheese you want over each patty (cheese is a very personal thing) and give it another 2 minutes to melt while the burgers finish cooking.

5 Assemble your gourmet fucking turkey burgers on the buns with the cranberry sauce, onions, and lettuce and try to convince your taste buds that this shit isn't bad for you.

DF **Serves 4**

12 ounces fresh cranberries

1 cup granulated sugar

1 cup orange juice or water

1 tablespoon olive oil

$1/2$ large sweet onion, sliced

$3/4$ teaspoon salt, divided

$1/4$ cup plain breadcrumbs

$1/4$ cup chopped fresh flat-leaf parsley

1 tablespoon chopped fresh sage

$1/4$ teaspoon freshly ground black pepper

1 pound ground turkey

Shredded white cheddar cheese

1 handful red leaf lettuce

4 hamburger buns

INDEX

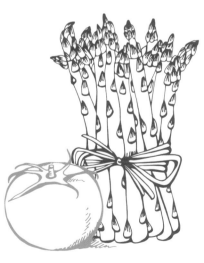

About the Author

ZOE GIFFORD is a freelance writer and food-lover who delights in a good recipe as much as a four-letter word. She lives in Chicago, Illinois, with her husband and three succulents.